Millom

remembered

Millom
remembered

BILL MYERS

TEMPUS

Frontispiece: Millom ironworkers about to tap a furnace in the 1960s. Shown are Harry Jones and slagger Tommy Butcher watched by (right) furnace foreman Harry Jones.

Overleaf: Hard at work in this 1963 photograph deep underground at Hodbarrow Mines are Peter Pietrzak and Jimmy O'Brien.

First published 2004

Tempus Publishing Limited
The Mill, Brimscombe Port,
Stroud, Gloucestershire, GL5 2QG
www.tempus-publishing.com

British Library Cataloguing in Publication Data.
A catalogue record for this book is available from the British Library.

ISBN 0 7524 3386 5

Typesetting and origination by Tempus Publishing Limited.
Printed in Great Britain.

Contents

Introduction

The quest for iron turned an isolated corner of the Duddon Estuary, on the Cumberland coast, into a place where fortunes could be made. Mine and ironworks investors, landowners and building speculators all helped turn the new Millom into a mini boom town. It would never grow to rival near-neighbour Barrow-in-Furness, but Millom must have been something special in the early days.

The pace of change in the 1860s and 1870s was simply frantic. Individual speculators built new homes with a combination of brick, slate and even boulders from the beach. By good fortune and the intervention of major landowners the new town was built to something approaching a pattern with none of the back-to-back slums seen in many Northern industrial communities.

Despite this, the new Millom and the rapidly expanding Haverigg had their fair share of social problems. Demand from incoming families to get any kind of roof over their heads was so great that there was little concern about the problems of living in what was essentially a giant, badly drained building site. Piped water, gas, proper roads and public services all had to wait until later.

People poured into the new community from all parts of the British Isles, including Ireland, Cornwall and the Isle of Man. In 1861 the Millom parish, including Thwaites and Ulpha, had fewer than 1,000 people. By 1871 Millom alone had a population of 4,307 and by the census of 1881 it had grown to 7,698. As the Victorian era came to a close in 1901 the town had 10,426 people.

By 1905 Millom and Haverigg had been transformed into a modern industrial, commercial and social centre with links throughout the world. There were shops and a co-operative society, public halls, churches and sports clubs. The grid pattern of Millom's town centre terraces was firmly established and building work was being completed on the area's biggest construction project, the sea defence Outer Barrier for Hodbarrow Mines. The population of both Millom and Haverigg in 1905 would have been at an all time high – possibly as high as 11,000 – swollen by more than 1,000 construction workers at Hodbarrow.

The following six chapters contain a mixture of historical notes and extracts from Furness-based newspapers. The author writes the 'Memories' page in the Barrow-based *Evening Mail* every weekday. The book draws on stories from the *Mail* – mostly under its earlier title of the *North Western Daily Mail* – and from a number of other Furness publications. These include the *Mail's* former sister paper, the *Millom News*, and long-vanished titles such as Soulby's *Ulverston Advertiser* and the *Millom Gazette*. Furness Newspapers, publishers of the *North West Evening Mail*, has kindly allowed the use of extracts from its archive editions for this project.

The articles have been chosen to give a taste of the great variety of topics touched on by newspapers during the development of Millom. They feature some of the great turning points in Millom's economic and social life. This includes royal visits, the opening of Millom Tannery and the new Elbeo factory; the closure of both Hodbarrow Mines and Millom Ironworks and the day Millom's soldiers marched off to the First World War.

Some of the early articles paint a vivid picture of Millom and Haverigg as frontier communities struggling to keep public order and maintain basic standards of building and health. Modern local newspapers try very hard to be neutral in reporting the news, leaving readers to form their own opinions. In the Victorian era the press was an integral part of the local political scene. The resident Millom reporter was frequently on his soap box shouting about lack of progress by officialdom or company managements. A flavour of this partisan news coverage comes across clearly in some of the early newspaper extracts.

The pictures in the book are from the author's own collection of 10,000 postcards and photographs covering the parts of old North Lancashire, Westmorland and Cumberland which became Cumbria in 1974. The selection is a wide one both in the range of topics covered and in the age of the pictures. The images go right up to the late 1960s. This was a time of vast change in Millom and the places and events captured on film from that period will be sharply remembered by most readers in Millom and Haverigg.

Exact dates and names have been given in the picture captions where they are known. All too often pictures pass through the generations and both the faces and the reasons why the pictures were taken are forgotten. If you have additional information about any of the photographs the author would be pleased to hear from you at the *Evening Mail's* Memories desk or by email at bill.myers@nwemail.co.uk.

Millom and Haverigg mark a series of major historical milestones in 2005. It is the 140th anniversary of the founding of Millom Ironworks, the sixtieth anniversary of the end of the Second World War and the 100th anniversary of the completion of the Hodbarrow Outer Barrier.

With the passing of the iron industry, the key reason for Millom being where it is has gone. The town is now looking forward to building a new role in the modern world. However, each new generation needs to know about the events and the people who helped forge Millom and Haverigg. They were men and women who knew all about hard work and had skills which have been put to use throughout the world. There should always be a bright future for people like that.

Bill Myers
October 2004

one

How it all Started

Multi-view postcards were popular with visitors to the town, offering at least five views for the price of one. This one is from around 1910 and features the Market Square.

How it all Started

The area of modern Millom was known in 1847 as Millom Below and was made up of the village of Holborn Hill and a scattering of detached houses. Its population in the 1841 census was given at 356. The Earl of Lonsdale, Anthony Cragg, and Joshua Myers were the largest landowners and Dalzell, Dickinson and Company had a brick and tile manufactory, near Holborn Hill.

The Mannix and Whelan History, Gazetteer and Directory of Cumberland, published in 1847, said Millom had a charter from 1250 for holding a market on Wednesdays and a fair for three days at the festival of the Holy Trinity. This extract describes the origins and early development of the Millom parish just before the quest for iron brought a major transformation to the coastal strip of West Cumberland and Furness:

The parish seems isolated by the sea, and the mountains on the west and north. The southern part is in general fertile, but a large portion of the north consists of wastes and pasture grounds. Thwaites chapelry affords excellent pasture, as also does Ulpha, which contains extensive woodlands, with some good grazing ground.

Limestone abounds in the parish, and is quarried in several places. Iron ore has been got at Hotbarrow and Millom Park, and smelted near the brook which still retains the name of Furnace-beck.

Mr Denton, who wrote in 1688, says that oak to the value of £4,000 had been cut down in the park to supply the forges in this parish. The iron ore shows itself most at a place called Waterblean. Copper ore has been obtained at different times, though seldom in sufficient quantities to repay the working; but a rich vein was discovered a few years ago, in the manor of Ulpha, and is now worked by George Harrison, Esq.

There are beds of slate in Millom Park, and in Thwaites, but they do not break sufficiently large for use.

The ruins of Millom Castle still stand guard over the main entrance to the town from the south. Its days of great influence over the lives of people in the district were long gone when this description was written for the Mannix and Whelan History, Gazetteer and Directory of Cumberland in 1847:

Millom Castle, of which there are considerable remains, was for many centuries the seat of the Lords of the seigniority of Millom, and though its venerable ruins have been neglected, they still point out its former strength and grandeur.

It was fortified and embattled in 1335 by Sir John Huddleston, in pursuance of the king's license, and was anciently surrounded by a park well stocked with deer and adorned with noble oaks, which it is said were cut down in 1690 by Ferdinand Huddleston, for the purpose of building a ship, and supplying fuel for his iron smelting furnace.

Nicholson and Burn wrote in 1774 that the park was 'well stocked with deer'. The late Earl of Lonsdale de-parked it in around 1802, when 207 deer were killed, and the venison was sold at between 2d and 4d per lb.

The principal part of the castle now remaining is a large square tower, formerly embattled. The moat is visible on the south and west sides; the principal entrance seems to have been at the west front, by a lofty flight of steps. In the wall of an out house are the arms of Huddleston, painted in proper colours, with the motto *Soli Deo honor et gloria*. A small part of the castle is now occupied as a farm house.

The seigniory of Millom is the most extensive lordship within the great barony of Egremont; it contains the parishes of Millom, Bootle, Corney, Waberthwaite, Whicham

Millom Castle is now partly ruined and partly a farmhouse. Engravings show it serving this dual role in the early eighteenth century. This Edwardian view up the castle steps gives an idea of how grand the old building must have looked in its heyday.

and Whitbeck, extending about eighteen miles in length, and about eight miles in breadth, but is divided into several manors, which are holden immediately of Millom, as Millom is of Egremont, with some difference of service.

This seigniority anciently possessed great privileges, its lords had the power of life or death, and enjoyed '*jura regalia*' in the six parishes forming their seigniority, and it was a special jurisdiction into which the sheriff of the county could not enter.

To commemorate the power of its lords, a stone has been recently erected with the following inscription: '*Here the Lords of Millom exercised Jura Regalia*'. It was given in the reign of Henry I by William Meschines, to the father of Godard de Bovil, (alias Godardus Dapifer) who gave to Furness Abbey a carucate of land with the appurtenances, called Monk Force.

The Boyvills, or Boisvilles, afterwards took the surname of de Millom, and held this lordship in their male issue from the reign of Henry I till the reign of Henry III, a space of 100 years, when their name and family ended in a daughter, Joan, who brought their inheritance in marriage to Sir John Huddleston, Knight, who was then lord of Anneys, near Millom, and could trace his ancestors for several generations before the Conquest.

His descendants possessed Millom for over 500 years; seven of the family were knighted for their valour, and one of them (Sir William) raised a regiment of foot soldiers at his own expense for the service of king Charles I. William Huddleston, the twenty-first of his family who held Millom, left two daughters, Elizabeth and Isabella, the former of whom was married to Sir Hedworth Williamson, Bart., who in 1774 sold the estate for little more than £20,000 to Sir James Lowther, Bart., whose descendant, the present Earl of Lonsdale, is now lord of the manor and owner of a great part of the soil.

Holy Trinity Church

Holy Trinity church, or The Old church, has long been regarded as one of the county's architectural gems but its glory was rather faded when described by writers for the Mannix and Whelan History, Gazetteer and Directory of Cumberland *in 1847.*

The Church of Millom, dedicated to the Holy Trinity, is situated in this township, close to the castle. It is a venerable edifice, consisting of a nave and chancel, a south aisle, and a modern porch, with a bell turret carrying two bells.

The circular-headed north door has been walled up, and most of the old windows have given place to modern un-ecclesiastical substitutes. Near the east window is a piscina, and at the west end is an octagonal stone font, ornamented with quartre-foils, and a shield charged with the arms of Huddleston and a label.

In the church is an ancient mural tablet, recording the names of several of the Huddleston family, and near to it is an altar tomb, ornamented with Gothic tracery, on which recline the effigies of a knight and his lady, in alabaster, much mutilated; and also the remains of a wooden effigy of a knight 'apparently of the fourteenth century', supposed to have been once clad in armour.

In the churchyard are the remains of a cross, the shaft of which bears four shields. It is grievous to see the neglected state of this ancient fabric, both internally and externally; its call for restoration seems alike unheeded by the Earl of Lonsdale and the inhabitants, whose duty it is to keep it in repair.

The benefice is now a discharged vicarage, in the patronage of the Duchy of Lancaster, but was rectorial till 1228, when it was given to Furness Abbey; one half of the revenue

Holy Trinity church has survived through hundreds of years of change. The interior was subject to major restoration at the hands of the Victorians. This view from around 1910 shows what to modern eyes is a rather unfamiliar position for the organ.

South West Corner and Old Organ, Holy Trinity Church, M

being appropriated by Walter de Grey, Archbishop of York, in 1230, for the maintenance of three chaplains in his cathedral.

It is valued in the king's books at £8 5s 8d, but was certified to the governors of Queen Anne's Bounty at the annual value of £26 1s 8d, and in 1835 at £189 a year. It was augmented about the year 1721, with £256 left by the Revd John Postlethwaite, master of St Paul's School, London, a native of this parish, and £200 obtained about the same time from Queen Anne's Bounty, both of which sums were expended in the purchase of an estate, called Fawcett Bank, near Sedbergh, in Yorkshire, which is now let for only forty guineas, though it once let for £70 per annum.

The Revd Henry Pickthall, BA, is the present vicar, having been inducted in 1836. The tithes, which belonged to the Earl of Lonsdale, have nearly all been redeemed by the different landowners.

The vicar has the patronage of the ancient chapel of Ulpha, but Thwaites chapel is in the hands of several landed proprietors. The tithes of Chapel Sucken Township were commuted in 1847, for a yearly rent charge of £128. The present vicarage house, and the glebe attached to it, was bought in 1781 for £240, of which £200 was obtained from Queen Anne's Bounty, and the remainder raised by subscription. It is situated in the township of Millom Above, distant about one mile from the church; the old vicarage house, which stood near to the church, having been pulled down during Cromwell's rebellion, 'lest the rebels should take refuge therein'.

13

Holborn Hill started life as a traditional fishing and agricultural village but gradually became part of the rapidly expanding new town of Millom. This view from around 1895 is taken below the Castle pub looking across to St George's church.

Town Emerges from Country Village

The early growth and development of Millom is really the story of Holborn Hill. Today it is just a street name but before the mid-Victorian growth of Millom Newtown the Main Street was the chief business and shopping area of the old Holborn Hill village.

When the railway arrived the new station was not called Millom but Holborn Hill and in earlier years the village was a popular last resting place for travellers before crossing the estuary sands.

The Pilot Inn at the top of the hill bears the inscribed stone 'William and Ann Barren live heare, who mostly keep good ale and beer, 1745. You that intend to cross ye sand, call here a gide at your command.'

P. Mannex and Company's 1882 trade directory *History and Directory of Furness and West Cumberland* still lists Main Street rather than Holborn Hill. It states that; 'The township contains the large and thriving village of Holborn Hill, which is said to have received its name from its resemblance to the well-known locality in London, and adjoining it is the new and rising town of Millom.'

At this time the village had its own school and places of entertainment. The directory said: 'The Central Public Hall, in Main Street, Holborn Hill, is fitted up with stage and other accessories for the performance of dramatic pieces.'

It also had its own places of worship: 'The Primitive Methodist Chapel, Bay View, Main Street, is a substantial stone building, erected in 1878, at a cost of £1,100, and presented to the connexion by the late Nathaniel Caine, Esq. of Broughton.' The building, which has now been demolished, had seats for 250 people.

There was an impressive range of shops and services listed in the 1882 directory, including Ann Birkett, midwife, of Main Street; Robert Black of the Ship Inn, Main Street; Thomas Bowness, grocer, of Main Street and William Bradley, builder, Holborn Hill. Also in the village were Isaac Brunton, beer house keeper, of the Commercial Inn,

Main Street; John Calder, the draper; Levica Carne; the dressmaker of Main Street, John Clarke, the police inspector and J. Casson, the nuisance inspector.

Robert Dixon was the village blacksmith, George Mackereth was the wheelwright and William Dobson ran the Red Lion beer house on Main Street. John Dodd the contractor and quarry master lived at Bay View, and Thomas Hall ran the Queen's Hotel on Main Street. William Lawrence was the Holborn Hill agent for the Reliance Mutual Life Association Society. Shoemaker William Porter worked from Main Street as did George Wilson the grocer, Jonathan Wilson the butcher and J. Stephenson the grocer.

Surgeon Percy Butler Stoney lived at Bay View along with builder Thomas Smith and E. Lilywhite the architect and surveyor. T. and W. Hodgson were soda water manufacturers and ale and porter bottlers on Main Street.

Bulmer's 1901 *History, Topography and Directory of Cumberland* said: 'As early as the year 1250 the Lords of Millom obtained a charter for holding a market at Holborn Hill on Wednesdays, and a fair of three days at the festival of Holy Trinity.' It also said: 'Millom Public Hall, Holborn Hill, was erected by a limited liability company, the foundation stone being laid by Lord Muncaster, September 9th, 1873.'

Holborn Hill also pioneered co-operative trading in the Millom area. The Holborn Hill Co-operative Society was established in 1870 and changed its name to the Millom Co-operative Society in 1887. By the time of the 1901 trade directory, Main Street was renamed Holborn Hill as the growth of Millom absorbed the old and once-separate village.

The New Town Emerges

The exact sequence of how the new Millom was built is difficult to trace. A few buildings, mainly churches and public buildings carry date stones but most streets can only be dated by their first mention in commercial listings of traders and prominent citizens.

Bay View, off Holborn Hill, Millom, was one of the streets built to cater for the growing town's more prosperous traders and professional people.

The Mannex *History and Directory of Furness and West Cumberland* shows that parts of the following streets had been completed by 1881: Albert Street, Bay View, Bedford Street, Borwick Rails, Devonshire Road, Duddon Street, Finch Street, Horn Hill, King Street, Lapstone Road, Lonsdale Road, Lord Street, Market Square, Market Street, Millom Road, Moore Cottages, Newton Street, Newton Terrace, Queen Street, Rottington Row, St George's Road, St George's Terrace, School Terrace, Steel Green Terrace and Victoria Street.

Some Millom buildings do carry date stones. The Bible Christian Sunday School in Newton Street had a sandstone block with the date 1894. It has now been demolished for housing. The Millom Market Hall and council offices were built in 1879 at a cost of £4,000. The Millom Club and Institute was built in 1882 at a cost of £1,600. It was bought by the council in 1891 for £1,800 to be turned into the town's public library and reading room. By 1906 it had 8,000 books and made 30,000 loans per year.

St George's church, Millom, was built in 1877 with the help of £7,186 donated by Millom Ironworks. The Roman Catholic Church of St James was built in 1868 and was enlarged in 1881. A house in Mainsgate Road has a stone tablet 'Myrtle Cottage 1889.' Millom Conservative Club in Lapstone Road has a date stone for 1894. The Millom fire station, facing up Earl Street, was opened in 1939. A house in Duke Street has a tablet reading 'H.F.F. 1894'.

The Millom Masonic Hall in Cambridge Street has a date stone saying: 'This stone was laid by Col F.R.S. Ewell 14 June 1901.' The Baptist church in Crown Street says:

Above: *Mainsgate Road, Millom, was on the main route to work for hundreds of Hodbarrow iron ore miners. This picture from the 1960s was taken before bungalows were built on open ground to the right.*

Right: *This postcard features one of the houses on Lapstone Road, Millom, in around 1910.*

Opposite: *Duddon Street, Millom, was demolished during clearance schemes in the 1970s. It gives an idea of how close slag tipping came to the bottom end of Millom Newtown.*

Above left: *Millom Market Square showing the West Country Hotel. The picture is from the late 1940s or early 1950s.*

Left: *A share certificate in the Millom Club and Institute Limited from 1885. The building later became Millom Public Library and the club moved round the corner from St George's Road to St George's Terrace.*

Below: *A horse and cart in Lapstone Road, Millom, on a postcard from around 1908.*

'Laid by T. Barlow-Massicks Esq. JP Aug 8th 1894'. One of the bank buildings facing into Market Square carries the date stone 'C.U.B. 1892'. The letters probably represent Cumberland Union Banking Company Limited.

Bricks for a Building Boom

You need a wide range of skills and many raw materials to construct a new town on open fields. Chief among the requirements was a reliable supply of building bricks, preferably without the high cost of transport on a heavy and bulky product. The Millom Brick Company rose to the challenge and the story of its formation was told in the Ulverston Mirror and Furness Reflector *on 14 July 1866:*

On Wednesday the shareholders in the Millom Brick Company Limited, together with a few friends, celebrated the opening of their new works by a dinner at the Station Hotel, Holborn Hill.

Previous to dining, the company visited the works and inspected the machinery, engine, and other plant, all of which is first-class.

The brick-making machine, which, of course, formed the chief attraction of the establishment, was described while in motion by Mr Matthews, managing director of the company, who very kindly conducted the visitors over the premises and explained the process of manufacture, from the time when the rough clay was received into the chamber until it was delivered in the shape of bricks.

This most ingenious and wonderful machine is one of Oates', of Birmingham, and the patent for Cumberland has been purchased by the Millom Brick Company.

The modus operandi may thus be briefly described: The clay is put into a powerful copper, in shape somewhat resembling a coffee-mill, in the inside of which is a working Archimedian screw, which presses the clay through an aperture into moveable dies.

The clay is then pressed out by means of eccentric motion on to endless belts, which carry the bricks complete to a couple of boys by whom they are loaded on barrows, and taken direct to the kilns, thus obviating the necessity common to hand-made bricks of being burnt, and effecting a saving of cost in production of fully 25 per cent as compared with the manual process.

While the moveable dies are pressing the clay into the form of bricks, a certain escape of clay at the back of the machines precludes the possibility of any breakage by reason of the enormous pressure that is employed to produce bricks from raw material in little more than a second.

The machine is capable of producing 2,000 bricks per hour. The average quantity produced daily is 15,000, or 90,000 per week.

In addition to the steam brick-making machine, there is also in the same department a powerful brick-pressing machine of the most novel construction for giving a fine finish to bricks to be used for frontal erections, and which will be found an admirable as well as cheap substitute for prepared stone.

The ordinary brick, as it leaves the brick-making machine close by, has only to be placed one at each end upon this pressing machine, which is also worked by steam power, and in an instant are produced two compressed bricks of the finest possible finish, one bearing the letters 'M.B. Co. L.' and the other those of 'H.H.', representing respectively the initials of the company and the name of the place of manufacture.

After the inspection of the works, the company sat down to a most excellent dinner provided by Mrs Beethom, of the Station Hotel. The chair was occupied by Mr Mathews, and the vice-chair by Mr Hudspith. A number of toasts and appropriate speeches were given.

Maintaining Law and Order

When the iron ore bonanza really got underway in the 1860s the area was still mostly farmland with too little of the housing and services needed to support the flood of people moving to Millom and Haverigg in search of work and a new way of life.

In 1866 work was under way to sink pit shafts at Hodbarrow Mines. The project brought in migrant workers from all over the British Isles. They were mostly living in what were little more than wooden huts. The new workers at Hodbarrow Mines and Millom Ironworks were in a strange new world. It was a tough life and they were tough people. Sometimes it all got just a little out of control!

As the summer temperatures rose so did tempers and at the start of July it all kicked off in spectacular fashion. The *Ulverston Mirror and Furness Reflector* of 7 July, 1866 recorded every detail for posterity.

Under the headline of 'Serious Riots at Haverigg' the report claimed: 'For the last few days Holborn Hill, Haverigg and the immediate neighbourhood have been in a state of terrible excitement and confusion, owing to the riotous conduct of a number of drunken men.'

There had been trouble in Haverigg before, always after the Saturday pay day. This time Saturday drinking, swearing and violence spilled into Sunday.

The report said: 'In the evening about 30 of them, as it would seem half-maddened with drink, wandered about the place watching for an opportunity of breaking the peace.' The lone upholder of law and order was PC Caseley, of Holborn Hill, Millom. He didn't stand a chance.

The paper stated: 'The constable was at once set upon without the least provocation having been given, beaten severely, and an attempt was made to drown him in Haverigg Pool. He was rescued, however, by some of the more civilised inhabitants, but not until he had received severe injuries.'

On Monday the violence continued, despite police reinforcements arriving from three police stations. The *Ulverston Mirror and Furness Reflector* wrote: 'The unruly mob then made a raid upon the public houses, the Rising Sun coming in for its share of unwished for attention.'

Landlord Mr Cleasby had seven gallons of rum stolen but he was not the type to grin and bear it. The paper wrote: 'Mr Cleasby obtained a double-barrelled gun, and with that loaded as a means of protection to himself and family, seems to have been able to keep the rascals at bay.'

Another publican, Myles Brockbank, sat with a loaded pistol for several days: 'On Wednesday, in pure self-defence, he was obliged to shoot one of the principal rioters, who we are told, had lifted up a knife for the purpose of stabbing him. The fellow was severely wounded.'

A street brawl later that day involved up to seventy people. Houses were broken open and villagers assaulted. The paper wrote: 'On Wednesday night to escape their violence, one woman, or more, was obliged to run naked from Haverigg to Holborn Hill, a distance of about a mile.'

A major flood defence project has changed the look of the bridge linking Haverigg to Concrete Square and the village cricket ground. This view of Poolside was taken in around 1947.

Summer weekends in Edwardian times saw the beach at Haverigg packed with visitors. This view is looking towards Concrete Square.

A quiet scene at Haverigg Pool in around 1910 with the River Lazy flowing into the Duddon Estuary.

A heavily pregnant woman was turned out of her house into the rain by the rioters. The action could not be allowed to continue so the Victorian equivalent of the riot squad was called in. After six days of turmoil the forces of law and order had sufficient numbers to take on the seventy-strong rabble with some chance of success.

The paper reported: 'On Thursday, Superintendent Little arrived with 30 men under his command, armed with cutlasses. They were kept under arms all night at Mrs Beethom's Station Hotel. The sight of policemen carrying swords seems to have done the trick and several arrests were made.'

It was left to the Carlisle courts to deal with them at the end of July. The *Ulverston Mirror and Furness Reflector* of 28 July, 1866 said eight men aged from twenty-one to forty were dealt with by Mr Baron Martin.

Mr M. Harrington, prosecuting, said: 'The officers stationed there had been doing their best to quell the riot during the whole week, but on Thursday it required 30 policemen to march up and down the town, armed with short cutlasses, to disperse the rioters.'

The jury found all the prisoners guilty. The judge said he had never heard a worse case and sentenced each to twelve months in jail with hard labour. Some lesser offences were dealt with by the Bootle petty sessions with fines of up to £10 and prison terms of up to two months being handed out.

Not a Drop to Drink

Millom grew at such a rapid rate that new houses outstripped the very limited capacity of natural fresh water sources and drainage provision. This had potentially serious public health implications and the newspapers of the 1870s often had complaints about living conditions in Millom and about outbreaks of illness, including scarlet fever. The Barrow Daily Times *of 6 October 1873, gave some hints at what life in the early days of Millom was like. It said:*
Little if anything has been done in the past in a sanitary point of view; and no movement seems to be at present on foot to lead to improvement. The houses are crowded; there is no regular water supply or systems of drainage; and it is time the public mind was thoroughly awakened so that a change might be effected.

The greater portion of the inhabitants, and particularly those who live in Newtown, are dependent for their water supply on two small springs, one of which, owing to mining operations, is often nearly dry; and both of which are a considerable distance from the bulk of the dwellings.

When the husband or the good wife reaches home after a day's toil it not infrequently happens that their recreation consists of a long journey to the spring to fetch water. Not only is there the journey to the springs in all kinds of weather, but often the wearisome waiting. All cannot be served at one and the same moment. The pails must take their turn.

Health and comfort cannot exist under such circumstances and anything approaching cleanliness is almost out of the question. Anyone at all acquainted with mining operations will readily understand what I mean. And yet these men who seem to be literally coated from head to foot with a substance, which were it only a little brighter in hue, would make them look something like boiled lobsters, must be content, when they get home to try and remove the disagreeable incrustation by means of a tumbler full of water.

Battling Over Water

Victorian newspapers did more than just report the news. They played an important role in highlighting social ills and pressing for change. This emotional piece from the resident Millom reporter for the Barrow Daily Times *described serious water shortages in an article published on Friday, 13 March 1874.*

It may be said that the good people who live here are truly a patient and long suffering people. Were there not a drop of water in this antithesis of paradise, I think they would take things as they came in a very easy-tempered, genial sort of way, and would possibly fold their arms and feel sweetly peaceful and resigned under the impression that by way of wholesome discipline it was a dispensation of providence that they should be very dry and stay dry, and that their daily inconveniences were in reality kind penances or mercies in disguise!

Otherwise how can this strange submissiveness, this sitting down coolly under intolerable burdens, be accounted for? Is it apathy with them, or with those to whom the lead in such matters has been given?

I think, had there not been this, under the circumstances, extraordinary apathy, the working men of the place would have wanted to know before this how it is the sanitary arrangements have been permitted to remain for so long a period in their present highly unsatisfactory and dangerous state, and, further, how it comes to pass that, now something 'official' is really to be done that something assumes the ludicrous shape of an Abyssinian pump simply by way of experiment.

I say ludicrous, because it is inadequate, and an arrangement which cannot do more than excite a smile of derision when it is remembered that this is a populous and very widely scattered place, and that the need is immediate and pressing.

To say the least, to not a few it will seem rather a cool proceeding to tell a working man living at one of the extreme points of Newtown, that if he wants water he must trudge with his buckets in all sorts of weather, and at all times, no matter at what inconvenience, to a pump which he would probably find besieged and completely invested by a frantic multitude.

The growing town of Millom built this reservoir at Basin Bank, off the Whicham Valley, to provide for its water needs.

And what will his supply be worth when he had obtained it amongst so many! Evidently a giant must bathe in a gill and quench his thirst with a thimbleful!

I need not say anything about the disastrous little civil wars which might take place near the said mighty institution, nor about the probable magisterial fines inflicted on the inevitable person called Jones, who was not noisy over his cups but over his buckets; but I will express the fear that when the course proposed has been carried into effect the majority of the people will be but little better off than they are now.

What is to be done should be done immediately, and should be more than something experimental. At the present time the position of the working man here is something like this: he is pretty certain to be found in a small and very much overcrowded house, built on marshy ground, and surrounded with reeking puddle holes and loathsome nuisances.

If he is a very fortunate man – mark that please – he will have the use of the rainwater, which finds its way into a water butt which is not perhaps very clean.

For the purposes of personal cleansing – and remember his occupation is that of a miner or ironworker – he must rely upon the supply of a butt, which after a few days dry weather entirely fails. And he is not the only sufferer.

Probably in his small rooms he lives with a wife and several children. Furthermore, his is not the only family in the house. There is another family, probably there are families, and every small room in the little house is crowded, and not used simply as a sleeping apartment, but as sitting room, dining room and general clatter, smudging and washing-up room!

Poor British workman! This is the kind of thing to strike against. And this patient creature, crouching down between burdens he need not bear, if he will not go altogether without water when his day's toil is ended, must rise to the full dignity of a water carrier, trudge a mile with his buckets to some deceptive ditch, where he can scoop up water which has been contaminated with animal matter and refuse. This is part of his daily life, it is his recreation.

One of the saddest sides of the picture, which would be intensely ludicrous in these times if it were not a serious matter, is that he is only able to obtain sufficient water for his most pressing needs, and that he is, struggle and toil as he will, unable to keep nuisances away from his premises, and to preserve the state of cleanliness he would.

The erection of an Abyssinian pump, which might be a great distance from his dwelling, however near it might be to some, would scarcely benefit him, and where there are so many to be supplied, the labour of fetching the water would be great.

It is stated that the temporary water supply scheme is to be supplemented by the employment of a number of water carts. Trifling as the arrangements might seem to outsiders, I hope it will be carried out immediately, as the people are suffering greatly from the want of water and if it is not supplied they will certainly be great sufferers and the present state of things will be greatly aggravated. There should, however, be no unnecessary delay.

As regards the disgraceful state of the puddle holes and the common land adorned with dirty pig sties, and covered with sewage matter in various parts of Newtown, to which I have before referred.

I hope the sanitary committee will take immediate and vigorous action. I am certain that delay is fraught with great evil and that any want of prompt and decisive action on the part of the authorities will be very reprehensible.

Oldest Woman in Town

Golden wedding anniversaries and birthday celebrations allow newspapers to look back on the past and shed light on unrecorded aspects of town life. An example of this was published in the Millom News *on 16 April, 1938 when Millom resident Mary Jane Middleton reached the age of 100. It said:*

Mrs Mary Jane Middleton, of 30 Newton Street, Millom, attained her 100th birthday on Sunday, when many messages of congratulation were received. In reply to these Mrs Middleton said 'Thank you very much' as if being a centenarian was an everyday event!

She sang *Safe in the arms of Jesus* which was played outside her home, and recognised *Abide with Me* (remarking it was a very old but beautiful hymn) which was sung by over 30 members of the Newton Street Methodist church in the street in the evening.

The church members also sang *Guide Me O Thou Great Jehovah*. The Revd E.W. Gibson, who conducted the choir, offered prayer. Mrs Middleton has been a staunch member of the church, formerly the Bible Christian church, for many years. In fact she worshipped in the same church as the famous Billy Bray, who she had frequently heard had built it, thus laying the foundation of the Bible Christian Association. Mrs Middleton remembered many things about the early days of that church association.

Mrs Middleton was very lively and cheerful when seen on her birthday by the paper's Millom representative, and was able to recall many events even up to 94 years ago.

Although practically blind, she is able to walk about the house. Beyond occasionally standing at her front door and sitting in the backyard on warm and sunny days, she has not been out of doors for many years. 'I am getting an old woman,' she explained.

She is a native of Frogpool, Cornwall, and was married at Redruth, to Mr Thomas Dunstone who was killed at the Hodbarrow Iron Ore Mines, Millom, 68 years ago. She subsequently married Mr Thomas Middleton, of Millom, who was well known in the town both as a stonemason and an authority on horses. Mr Middleton, who died about 1900, helped to build St George's church, the market hall, the council chambers, and several other buildings in Millom. There were eight children of the two marriages, five of whom are still alive. There are six grandchildren and three great-grandchildren.

'So I am a hundred. Do I look it?' she asked with a smile. 'I am sorry I cannot see, but I think I'm an old woman.' After saying this she laughed heartily and said 'Mind you, I am an old woman and don't remember very many things.'

Mrs Middleton, however, clearly illustrated her wonderful memory when she recounted an episode of her early life. 'I can remember being about six or seven years of age when I first started to work,' she said. 'I started work picking copper ore and I got threepence a day for working from seven in the morning to half-past five in the evening. My work consisted of sitting at a table on which was placed a lot of washed copper ore from which I had to separate the good from the bad. It is a happy memory,' she said.

Mrs Middleton followed her husband to Millom about 1863 when she came with her mother and two small children. 'We went from Redruth to Penzance by train and to Liverpool by boat. The train brought us to Millom from there. Millom then was only a small place for the iron ore mines had only just started. There were a few houses in Newton Street, King Street and Albert Street in those days. Houses were being built very quickly.

'I remember how we used to get water. We had to go with pails to a place now known as Dowbiggin's field and get water out of the dyke, while we had to pay for water which we wanted for drinking purposes. There was a spring on the Marsh and we had to go down between the tides to get our pails full. How different from today,' she smilingly observed.

Mrs Middleton went on to say her first husband was killed by a fall of ore a few months before their daughter Emily (Mrs Hand, who resides in Sheffield) was born.

'I had been content all my life,' she answered to a question as to what was the probable cause to her living to such a great age, 'but perhaps God has kept me for purpose. I am happy.' She smiled and closed her eyes.

A wedding reception at the Queen Street Methodist church, Millom, in the 1890s.

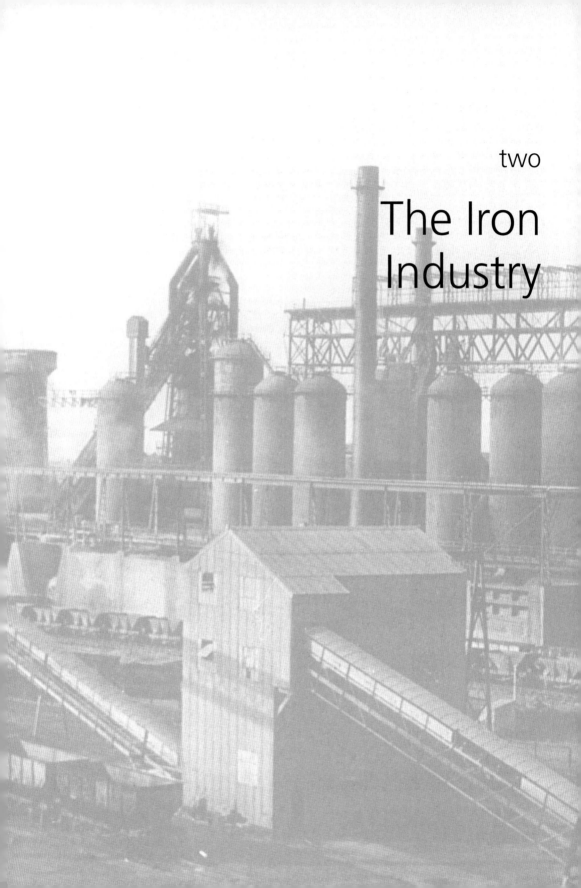

two

The Iron Industry

Above: *This view from around 1940 gives some idea of the scale of mine subsidence which tore apart the Hodbarrow Inner Barrier, built in 1890.*

Opposite above: *A group of Hodbarrow miners pose for a photograph around the time of the First World War.*

Opposite below: *Share certificates in Hodbarrow Mines were valuable things. At one stage the company was so profitable that shareholders were being paid a dividend every month. This un-issued example dates to around the time of the First World War.*

Searching for Iron Ore

The story of serious attempts to commercially exploit iron ore at Hodbarrow, Millom, starts in 1855 when the Earl of Lonsdale granted a licence to search for minerals. Cornishman John Barratt led the exploration in the area around Towsey Hole at Hodbarrow Point.

Work to sink a shaft was under way the same year and iron ore was found in 1856. This was no bonanza but what ore was raised held out sufficient promise to make the search for substantial reserves worth persevering with.

The early shareholders in the mine were John, William and James Barratt; Liverpool iron merchant, Nathaniel Caine and his brother William; Ulverston solicitor, Thomas Woodburne; Liverpool accountant, John Bewley and Coniston surgeon, R.T. Bywater.

By 1861 sufficient ore had been indicated by test bores towards Redhills Quarry to give the partners confidence to sign a lease on the mine for twenty-one years. Within a year the ten or so miners working at Hodbarrow has grown to nearly thirty. A new shaft and underground levels were being driven and work begun to build a pier to ship out ore from Crab Marsh Point. In 1863 John Barratt, Nathaniel Caine and Thomas Woodburne became the first directors.

The pace of activity was picking up all the time and in 1864 the mines were profitable, one million tons of ore had been discovered and more than 150 men were working

CERTIFICATE Nº 52   SHARES.

The Hodbarrow Mining Company Limited.

INCORPORATED APRIL 30TH 1888.

CAPITAL ₺550,000

DIVIDED INTO 50,000 SHARES OF ₺8 EACH. AND 15,000 SHARES OF ₺10 EACH.

This is to Certify that _____

is the Registered Proprietor of _____ fully paid
Shares of ₺8 each numbered as per margin in The Hodbarrow
Mining Company Limited subject to the Company's Memorandum
and Articles of Association.

Given under the Common Seal of the Company
the _____ day of _____ 19__

_____
_____ } DIRECTORS.

_____ SECRETARY.

NOTE—NO TRANSFER OF THESE SHARES OR ANY PORTION OF THEM WILL BE REGISTERED UNLESS ACCOMPANIED BY THIS CERTIFICATE.

underground in what became known as the Old Mine. During 1867 and 1868 the first parts of what became the New Mine were discovered near Steel Green. It was eventually proven to be a huge expanse of ore up to 100ft thick.

This New Mine was brought into production in 1874. By the 1880s more than 1,000 men and boys were employed at Hodbarrow. Underground work on this scale inevitably led to major subsidence of the overlaying ground. This threatened the existence of the entire mining operation due to the risk of seawater flooding the workings.

After a new lease was agreed with Lord Lonsdale in 1888, work started on a sea wall, known as the Inner Barrier. It was designed by Sir John Coode to safeguard the mine workings and allow the exploitation of another five million tons of ore lying closer to the coast. Work on the wall was completed in 1890 but it quickly became a victim of the same subsidence which led to it being built in the first place. The warning sign came on 17 May 1898, when wet sand got into the workings and when the tide went out it revealed a forty-yard-wide hole in the ground just 100 yards from the face of the Inner Barrier. Four days later part of the wall subsided.

It was obvious another, much more substantial, barrier was needed. Work on this cost £600,000 and was completed in 1905.

The last of the major new ore bodies was found at Moorbank, near Haverigg, in January 1925. Moorbank Pit was the last to raise ore at Hodbarrow until the mines closed in 1968.

During the 113-year history of Hodbarrow Mines a total of twenty-five million tons of iron ore was raised to the surface. Between 1905 and 1909 the mine was producing more than a half-million tons of ore per year. The record production came in 1907 with 545,736 tons.

After 1932 the mines never exceeded 100,000 tons per year and after 1954 totals never reached 50,000 tons again. In 1967, the final full year, the tonnage had fallen to 27,924 and it was obvious the end was near.

Today the two giant sea defence barriers and the flooded expanse of Hodbarrow Lagoon remain to give some idea of the size and former importance of Hodbarrow Mines.

For a comprehensive survey of the mine's development readers should refer to *Cumberland Iron, the Story of Hodbarrow Mines 1855-1968* by A. Harris.

Holding Back the Sea

Hodbarrow Outer Barrier was the biggest civil engineering project seen in Millom. Its scale was enormous, as was its importance to the prosperity of Millom and Haverigg. The barrier celebrates its centenary in 2005. Here is how the Millom Gazette, *of Thursday 20 April 1905 described the excitement as the work was finally completed:*

On Thursday in last week the last block of the Hodbarrow Outer Barrier was laid by the chairman of the Hodbarrow Mining Company, Mr Harry Arnold.

This marks the completion of the great works which the Hodbarrow Mining Company have had in hand for the last five years, a work of a magnitude which it falls to the lot of a few private firms to have to face.

Its history will be too fresh in the minds of our readers to need recapitulation here, but it may be remarked that it is not the first sea wall which the company has erected, the Old Sea Wall being completed some 15 years ago.

Work under way on the timber core structure for the Hodbarrow Outer Barrier, around 1901.

This wall only reclaimed a relatively small area but it enabled the company to win a vast amount of the valuable iron ore deposit and for several years it answered well the purpose for which it was designed.

Then came the famous 'break' when it looked for a brief time as if Hodbarrow and Millom might be wiped out by the watery element which the company has had to fight for so long.

Happily that catastrophe was averted by the energetic measures that were adopted. A new wall had for some time previously been talked of, but from this time onward it became an imperative necessity.

The borings which had been continuously made showed that the ore deposit extended seaward to great thicknesses, and to win this – indeed, to keep the mines going – the new sea wall loomed ahead as a problem that would have to be tackled at an early date, and today we see the completion of the work, the magnitude of which is due to the joint efforts of the engineers (Messrs Coode, Son & Matthews) and the contractors (Sir John Aird & Co.) combined with the enterprise of the Hodbarrow company, and it is confidently anticipated that the protection thus afforded to the mines will be sufficient to ensure their successful working for many years to come.

Notwithstanding the unfortunate state of the weather in the morning, there was a

This quiet pastoral view of a cart stacked high with hay was taken on the Hodbarrow Outer Barrier soon after it was opened in 1905. Mine subsidence and the end of pumping with the closure of the iron ore mines, means water laps against the inner side of the barrier today.

fairly large gathering of guests who had been invited to be present on the interesting occasion. Arriving by the midday trains, conveyances were in waiting to take them to the Hodbarrow offices.

The display of bunting here betokened that something unusual was in hand and there was a little crowd of sightseers assembled to catch what at best was certainly a distant view.

Close by the officers a fussy little engine looking very gay and proud in all the smartness that a plenteous use of flags could afford, attached to a small string of one closed and three open wagons was impatiently waiting.

We take our seats at about 12.30, and after some shrill whistling on the part of the lusty little locomotive, the guard mounts the rear wagon, waves his hand to the driver, and we begin to run 'tender first' in the direction of Haverigg.

Arrived opposite the road to the 'Frying Pan', we stop, our guard dismounts and alters the points, and then we go, the engine now hauling instead of pushing us, along the new wall. Here the massive concrete boulders which are to act as 'wave breakers' are seen to great advantage, and the solidity of the work is apparent.

We steam steadily along, with the Irish Sea lying calm at our feet, until we came to the middle of the wall, where we came to a stop and 'detrain'.

Facing us is the big travelling crane which has just brought its labours to an end and by its side is a raised dais carpeted with some crimson material and surrounded with a wooden framework which has a bright appearance by reason of the numbers of flags fluttering in the breeze, which by the way, we now find to be considerably stronger than we had found before we started on our round tour.

Under the guidance of Messrs Vaughan and Barratt the party make a short excursion to the front of the wall to view the works as seen from the seaward side.

Then we all make our way to the enclosed dais, where the huge block of concrete is suspended ready to be lowered into position. In the middle of the block is a handsome slab of polished red granite, specially sent to the Hodbarrow company by the contractors from Egypt, this being a piece of stone from the Assouan dam. It bears the inscription: Hodbarrow Mines. This block was laid by Harry Arnold Esq., chairman of the Hodbarrow Mining Company Limited, on the completion of the Outer Barrier. 'Commenced April 1900. Cedric Vaughan and William Barratt, managing directors. Coode, Son and Matthews, engineers. John Aird and Company, contractors.'

John Matthews produced a silver trowel for Harry Arnold to lay the final stone and John Aird handed him a mallet to tap it into place. A luncheon was held at the Hodbarrow offices, Steel Green.

The newspaper gave a detailed description of what it had taken to build the huge barrier. It said:

The new or Outer Barrier encloses an area of 170 acres, its length is one mile and one-third, it has an extreme height of 40ft, the depth of water alongside at high water being 20 to 25ft, and its greatest width is 210ft at the base and 83ft at the top.

The structure differs from that of 1890 in that instead of being a rigid wall it is a flexible embankment, this form having been adopted in order that if at any time subsidence should take place in the ground beneath the barrier it also should subside and accommodate itself to the contour of the ground, when by adding material to the superstructure, its efficiency as a protection to the mines would be maintained.

The embankment consists of two parallel banks of rough limestone with a filling of clay between. The outer and larger bank is protected from the heavy stroke of the sea by a coating of concrete blocks, each weighing 25 tons, deposited irregularly, which breaks up the waves as they strike the barrier.

An important feature of the work is the method by which the percolation of seawater either through or beneath the barrier has been provided against. For this purpose a watertight cut-off has been formed in and under the heart of the embankment.

In the centre of the ordinary clay filling a wall of specially milled or puddled clay is constructed, and where there existed, beneath the foundations of the barrier, a bed of clay at so great a distance below the surface, this wall was carried down and joined to the natural clay. Where the natural clay bed was at too great a depth to be reached in this manner the lower portion of the cut-off was formed by means of grooved and tongued close timber piling, the points of the piles being driven down into the clay.

Where, again, no clay existed, or was at too low a level to be reached in a satisfactory manner by timber piling, steel sheet piling, ranging in length according to circumstances, the longest being 35ft, was driven. Of this latter work there is no less than seven-eights of a mile, forming a continuous steel diaphragm of that extent.

There is thus a water-tight cut-off extending from about 32ft below the surface of the foreshore to 5ft above high water level, or nearly 60ft in height. At the centre of the barrier four sluiceways are provided, by means of which any water that may accumulate in the reclaimed area (and in time of heavy rain this is a considerable quantity) can be discharged during the period when the tide has receded from the face of the embankment.

An idea of the magnitude of the work may be gathered from the following particulars of the quantities of material used in its construction. One-and-a-half million tons of limestone, nearly one million tons of clay, 150,000 tons of concrete, 4,400 tons of steel, and 100,000 cubic feet of timber.

The exclusion of the sea from so large an area involved special arrangements for closing the barrier. This important and special feature of the work was, however, carried out with the precision as arranged, and was attended with the most satisfactory results.

The first sod was turned on 27 April 1900 by Mr Harry Arnold, chairman of the Hodbarrow Mining Company, and the sea was excluded from the reclaimed area by the closing of the barrier on 20 July 1904. Since the latter date the work necessary to finish the structure has proceeded, and the barrier is now completed, having thus occupied just five years from start of finish. The last block was laid by the chairman on the 13th instant.

Houses for Iron Workers

The Hodbarrow Mining Company could never have foreseen its role as a major landlord in Millom and Haverigg. That role was largely forced on it by the need to house the workers required to sink and then exploit the iron ore workings. Whole families came to Millom looking for a new life. Many with a mining background came from Ireland, Cornwall, West Cumberland, Wales and the Isle of Man.

By October 1886 the Hodbarrow company had tenants in more than 100 properties. These were listed as nos 1-52 Concrete Square, Haverigg; nos 53-64 Caines Cottages, Haverigg; three tenants at the Baptist Chapel, Haverigg; twenty-six tenants at Steel Green Cottages; five tenants at Steel Green; five tenants, including one in the office, at Steel Green Terrace; six tenants, including the hospital and Whitehouse, at Mainsgate; six tenants at Hodbarrow; Leyfield House, home of director Cedric Vaughan; and Mains, Millom, home of harbourmaster William Morgan.

The last part of Steel Green Terrace to be demolished in 1983. The former Hodbarrow Mines offices are to the right, now the Commodore.

During Victorian times people lived close to their work, no matter how noisy, dirty or dangerous it might be. These houses, now demolished, are at Borwick Rails. They were right next to the main entrance to Millom Ironworks.

By 1890 the housing stock had been expanded by building what became known as the Company Houses. The eighty-eight new houses were in Oxford Street and Surrey Street, Millom. The contract went to Millom builder William Park. The first of the forty-four Surrey Street houses were due to be ready for tenants in March 1889. A total of 140 people applied to become tenants. Rents for the new houses were £8 10s (£8.50) a year. A notice survives from 1893 showing how Hodbarrow Mines was keen to impose its authority on tenants. It said:

'In consequences of the dirty condition of several backyards of houses belonging to us, we have determined to notify to our tenants that no pigs, or other animals, ducks, geese or poultry of any description are to be kept within 30 yards at least of the dwellings, and all wooden buildings erected in the yards must at once be removed except such as sanctioned by the company through their inspector, and furthermore, all drains must be kept properly cleansed and backyards free from refuse of any kind.'

The best known of the housing projects built for the mining company was Concrete Square at Haverigg. The cottages were started in 1872 and took two years to complete. They were high-tech for the time and were designed by Lewis Hornblower of Liverpool. His novel building technique was to encase hollow earthenware tiles or pipes within the concrete. The five blocks of houses at Concrete Square were finally demolished in 1973.

By the 1950s mining had gone from being an industry that nearly every Millom family had an involvement in to being something of a novelty. Most younger people had no experience of the red-stained life underground so the Evening Mail *of Thursday, 29 March, 1951 gave readers a taste of a miner's life under the headline 'Winning iron ore from Millom mine'. The report said:*

We wanted to find out all about an iron ore miner's job and there was only one way in which it could properly be done – to go underground. So we visited Hodbarrow Mines at Millom, where lie rich deposits of iron ore, and were taken down by Mr R.B. Davis, the manager.

First we put on working clothes, which include a white linen skullcap worn under the helmet to prevent the red dust from getting into our hair, and we carried a small carbide lamp. In Wellington boots we felt very much the part as we made our way to Moorbank Shaft where the cage was waiting.

The iron gate was slammed behind us and we were on the way, assisted by a 240hp winding engine, down the shaft which is 16ft in diameter, through ground that was frozen before the shaft could be sunk. Small though the cage seemed to our eyes, it holds eight men and accommodates one ton of ore. The ride down to the 90 fathoms level was smooth and similar to a lift.

As we descended, that dank smell which is met with underground assailed our nostrils, but the mine was much better ventilated than coal mines we had visited. The temperature down below was equable – indeed in winter the mine is warmer than above ground and conversely, cooler in summer. The main electricity-lit haulage road is 7ft high and 10ft wide and is partly lined with concrete.

We took a look first at the main pump house which had been cut out of solid rock and lined with concrete. Here are four electric pumps, capable of pumping to the surface

The Hodbarrow Mining Company provided company housing for its employees at a variety of sites in Millom and Haverigg. This group of cottages are at Concrete Square, Haverigg, on a picture dated 1924.

A Hodbarrow iron ore miner at work, around 1950.

2,000 gallons of water per minute, to be discharged into the sea. The actual flow of water from the workings is normally 450 gallons per minute. By this time we had overcome most of our initial feeling of trepidation, so we made our way along the road, past the rushing water, to the workings.

Not even a complete novice, Mr Davis told us, can get lost in the mine. By following the flow of water he will eventually reach the shaft. That was a consoling thought. Then our troubles started. To get to the workings we had to climb up a ladder which disappeared into the darkness in an alarming sort of way. Having only my lamp to carry, I was lucky, but it was tough on my photographer companion who was encumbered with a camera and flash outfit. The ladders were slippery and we were relieved to get up, and having got up, come safely down again.

We stopped to have a word with Jack Savage and Tom Park, who had just blasted and were filling the ore into a small bogie, which we were surprised to learn, held half-a-ton of broken ore. The ore is soft and greasy, and left a coating on our hands when we touched it. The quality of the Hodbarrow ore is the best in the country – equal to many imported ores – and is in great demand.

Down the ladder again, and along the tunnel cut through the rock, splashing through water – those Wellingtons proved useful – to the next working, then up another ladder where I got temporarily stuck. Here we found Bill Brown boring holes for blasting while his mate, Harold Shepard – the miners work in pairs – was laying down boards.

Left: *Two Hodbarrow iron ore miners push a bogie filled with ore, around 1950.*

Below: *A group of Hodbarrow miners with their stiffened felt hats and tallow candles. This picture would have been taken around the time of the First World War.*

This group of Hodbarrow miners took the chance for a break from their hard labour, around 1890.

The purpose of this is that the ore which has been blasted falls on to the boards and the smooth surface makes shovelling – or spading as it is called – easier. Roland (Ginger) Birkett, the Haverigg bowler, was busy at the next working securing his timber, assisted by Peter Pietzak, a Pole.

The timbering is very well done in this mine and the method used at Hodbarrow for shoring has been copied in Africa and India. Hodbarrow men were in great demand for overseas mines to show the natives their method of timbering.

We walked up to the 60 fathoms level where we saw the diesel locomotive which is used to bring the ore to the shaft on a 22in gauge railway. The interesting point about the loco is that it was the first diesel to be used in an iron mine in this country. As Hodbarrow is free from gas, carbide lamps are used and the men can have a smoke while they are underground.

The workings are comfortable and offer space for standing up. When the ore is extracted the void left is filled with sand washed down a borehole from the surface, then the water drains off and leaves the working safely packed. This is an expensive method of working but is extremely safe.

I was struck at all the workings we visited by the friendly spirit which permeates the mine and the relations between management and men are good. I was told that in some cases it was the third generation of miners who were working for the company. These men are doing a vital job of work; they are producing much-needed ore, and in so doing are keeping down imports and assisting the export trade. The ore mined at Hodbarrow is used at Millom, Barrow, Workington, Sheffield and Manchester, among other places.

We came to the surface, changed and washed. Then before leaving Hodbarrow we looked over the workings to the great Outer Barrier built to protect the mine, and finished after five years' work in 1905. When we did leave it was with a feeling of respect for the men who toil underground to mine the ore which keeps ironworks busy in many parts of the country.

End of an Era

The announcement that Hodbarrow Mines was to close after more than a century came in the North Western Evening Mail *on 10 October, 1967. The report said:*

Hodbarrow Iron Ore Mines at Millom, which have produced some of the finest ore in Europe for over a century, will close in March next year. More than 100 men at the mines will have to seek new jobs. Not all of them may be absorbed in Millom's industries.

Left: *This miner is shown at work around the time of the First World War. He is filling an ore bogie with ore drawn down from a hopper linked to a higher working level.*

Opposite: *Moorbank Pit took ore from the last major find at Hodbarrow. It was the last pit working when the mines were closed. In the background is Steel Green village.*

The closure was announced today by the Millom Hematite Ore and Iron Co. Its managing director, Mr D.R.G. Davies, told an *Evening Mail* reporter that the mines, which opened in 1856, are closing through exhaustion of deposits.

He said the closedown would be not later than 31 March, 1968, but stressed that it would have no effect on production at Millom Ironworks.

At the turn of the century the mines were yielding half-a-million tons a year. Output has dropped to 30,000 tons in recent years. Mr Davies said the actual date of closure in March would depend on output maintained in the intervening period.

He said: 'The mines were at their peak some 50 years ago, but with progressive working, extraction has become more difficult and recently the mine became uneconomical. The workable ore is now virtually exhausted and the company has regretfully come to the conclusion to close. This conclusion has only been arrived at after a thorough investigation in which the mineral owner, Lord Lonsdale, has played an important part, including a search for alternative methods of extracting the residual iron ore deposits.'

Mr Davies said the company would not be able to offer alternative employment to most of the 135 men, who include miners, shot firers and craftsmen. He said: 'Strenuous efforts are being made to enlist government support for local projects to provide suitable jobs.'

The company would be able to absorb a very small number of the men. At present Millom Ironworks was importing 100,000 tons of ore through Barrow Docks. Imports would be increased as a result of the Hodbarrow closure. Future requirements of home ore would be fully met from the Florence-Ullcoats mine at Egremont.

Talks were held yesterday between Mr Davies and Mr Thompson Reed of the National Union of General and Municipal Workers and trade union representatives on the Board of Conciliation for the Cumberland Iron Ore Trade.

Mr Davies said that for more than a year they had seen the closedown coming. He said: 'This has been a wonderful mine, but like all mines nearing the end of their life, the cost of extracting ore becomes very much higher. Lord Lonsdale has played an important part in exploring other methods of extracting residual ore, but the mine is almost exhausted'.

Turning Ore to Iron

Millom had a proud, century-long tradition of making iron but was lucky to even get an ironworks as the original plan was to build at Whitehaven.

The Cumberland Mining and Smelting Company Limited was formed with the intention of building blast furnaces on a site at Mirehouse, just south of West Cumberland port and coal mining centre. Talks were opened over a lease with a major Whitehaven land owner, the Earl of Lonsdale, in 1865. The talks stalled and the company had more luck with negotiating a lease at Millom.

Two furnaces were built and first produced iron in 1867. Another pair of furnaces quickly followed. In the early days Millom was able to produce around 150 tons per week from each furnace. Rapid developments in blast furnace design made the original furnaces outdated and in 1874 they were replaced by four of greater capacity and equipped with regenerative hot blast stoves using gas which had been allowed to go to waste.

In 1890 the Millom and Askam Hematite Iron Company Limited was formed to buy and join the Millom Ironworks of the Cumberland Mining and Smelting Company Limited, the Askam Ironworks of the Askam and Mouzell Company Limited, plus their hematite ore mines, limestone quarries and other assets. At this time the Millom company had six blast furnaces and was working iron ore mines at Whicham, near Millom, and Highfield, near Dalton. The Askam works had four furnaces.

The new company had a share capital of £250,000 in £10 shares and they issued five per cent debentures for a further £150,000. The new firm's directors were company chairman A.J. Mundella, MP, deputy chairman and managing director T. Barlow-Massicks, JP, Herbert Campbell, Harry Cook, George E. Holt, William Jacks and Greville R. Vernon. Thomas Barlow-Massicks had been the managing director of both the Millom and Askam companies prior to amalgamation. The two works were said to have the capacity of producing 250,000 tons of pig iron a year and the prospectus indicated expected earnings would be sufficient to yield a 12 per cent dividend on the ordinary shares, but the distribution would not exceed 10 per cent until the debentures had been redeemed.

The Millom and Askam works were both kept in operation and eventually a new, mechanically-charged blast furnace was built at Askam to replace the four old hand-charged furnaces. When recession hit the iron industry at the end of the First World War it was decided to close the Askam works and concentrate on the development of the Millom furnaces. The Askam works were finally demolished in 1938.

By 1918 Millom had installed new modern-design stoves, pig breakers, turbo-blowers, turbo-alternators, Stirling water tube boilers and Halberg-Beth gas cleaning plant. Another major reconstruction scheme in 1932 included the building of three blast furnaces, each capable of producing 300 tons of pig iron per day. Stoves were rebuilt to

A steam locomotive on the Millom Ironworks line which linked to Millom railway station. This picture dates from the 1960s.

operate with clean gas and Theissen washers were introduced with a capacity of two million cubic feet. Extra electricity generating plant was introduced and the boiler plant was updated to give an extra 66,000lbs of steam per hour. The most important development in 1932 was the installation of a sinter plant with a daily output of between 500 and 600 tons.

In the early 1930s Millom took over the North Lonsdale Iron and Steel Company Limited which had a blast furnace at Ulverston. The furnaces there had not been modernised, although new blowing engines had recently been installed with further improvements in mind. Operations were not economic and the plant was closed down, being restarted for a short time in 1940 when there was a national shortage of iron.

Millom's first pig casting machine came in 1898 and was of the Uehling type – the first of its kind in Great Britain. Traditional sand casting remained in use at Millom until 1939 when it was superseded by a new pig casting machine of the link belt type. This produced pigs, or ingots, of convenient shape and regular size. This made them easier to store and ship. The standard iron ingot became established at 42lb. A smaller pig casting machine for refined iron was added to the foundry in 1954.

With the end of the nationalised iron industry the Millom empire was acquired by the Millom Hematite Ore and Iron Company Limited and in 1959, through an exchange of shares, it was taken over by the Cranleigh Group which operated the plant until closure.

There were a number of big changes in 1960. A modern pig casting machine of the Ashmore, Benson & Pease fixed roller type was introduced, along with a new boiler plant. The same year saw the blowing in of the new Number 1 furnace – the largest of its type in Great Britain. Installed by Marley and Company of Workington, the new furnace stood 170ft high with a hearth diameter of 20ft. It could produce 700 tons of

A very busy scene at Millom Ironworks with rows of rail wagons waiting to be filled.

iron per day. The hot metal was tapped from the furnace into 70-ton capacity ladles and taken to the pig casting machines or to the foundry.

The Randolph Coke and Chemical Works at Evenwood in County Durham was added to the Millom-based group in 1963 and the Barrow Ironworks at about the same time.

By the end of the 1950s the Millom Ironworks site had nearly thirty miles of railway track to move ore, coke and limestone.

Millom's ore crushing, screening and stockpiling plant was built in 1958 by Sheepbridge Equipment to ensure the charge of material to the furnaces was of a consistently high standard. Hopper wagons filled with iron ore were shunted to sidings at the plant and were run by gravity to wagon tippers. The ore was weighed on a 35-ton Avery weighing machine and fed to a Kennedy gyratory crusher. Crushed ore went across Kennedy Twodeck vibrating screens where heat was used to dry the ore and different-sized wire meshes sorted it.

The smaller fines were removed to the sintering plant and the rest was now ready for the blast furnaces. The ore crushing and screening plant could cope with up to 300 tons of ore per hour. The sinter plant turned tiny pieces of ore which would have been waste into a useable material for the furnaces. The plant could produce 3,400 tons per week by working a two-shift system, or up to 5,000 tons per week using three shifts.

Millom Ironworks built a large foundry in 1949 to handle high-grade castings – including ingot moulds and refined iron and bar iron. The foundry was 660ft long, 70ft high and 60ft long. It had two cold-blast cupolas, three Tropinas converters, a pig casting machine for refined iron, an automatic sand mixing mill and pattern shop. Ingot moulds of up to 20 tons could be produced.

Millom also had its own laboratory, staffed by metallurgical chemists to study the content of Millom products and maintain quality control. The range of ingredients and traces they had to control within the iron included phosphorus, sulphur, manganese, silicon, molybdenum, nickel, cobalt and aluminium. As early as 1885 customers had started to specify pig irons by exact content analysis and Millom was among the pioneers in working to strict specifications.

Ore from Millom Ironworks eventually came from all over the world. In the early 1870s the company established its own hematite iron ore mine at Whicham, between Kirksanton and Silecroft. It never became a major success. Around 1897 mining was undertaken at Ullcoats and in 1905 Millom acquired the Ullbank Mine, also near Egremont. In later years other ores came to Millom from Africa, Portugal and Spain.

Apart from its ownership of local ore deposits, the Millom and Askam Hematite Iron Company Limited had a half interest in an ore property in Spain and in 1925 became the sole owner of the Alquife Mines and Railway Company together with a large ore loading terminal at the nearby port of Almeria. After the nationalisation of the iron and steel industry in 1951 this property was hived off. Later the Spanish properties were sold to the Altos Hornos Company of Bilbao.

Years of Profit

The First World War brought great prosperity to Millom Ironworks and the government put pressure on companies to raise output of vital war materials needed for shells and huge plates for warships and submarines. This was a time of rising profits, rising food prices and rising demands for trade union rights and higher wages. The North Western Daily Mail *of Saturday, 20 November, 1915, gave an idea of how well things were at Millom. It said:*

The ordinary shareholders of the Millom and Askam Hematite Iron Company are to receive a dividend of 10 per cent this year, providing the recommendation of the directors is approved at the annual meeting to be held at Preston on Monday. None of those who have invested their money, or some of it, in this prosperous concern is likely to cavil at the results of the year's working as contained in the annual report, or at the proposal for the distribution of the profits, which amount to the handsome sum of £78,393.

This is nearly double the profits for 1913-14, but about £2,000 less than in 1912-13, when a dividend of 12 per cent was paid. However, the balance sheet this year is one of the best of recent years, and must give every satisfaction to those interested. After all, 10 per cent is a nice little bit to be going on with, and the company is wisely adding to its financial stability each year.

Again £25,000 is transferred to the reserve fund, which now stands at £75,000, while the substantial sum of £25,000 has been written off for depreciation. The sum carried forward to the next account is close on £10,000, and the prospects of the company, so far as they can be gauged in these days of strife and uncertainty, seem to be entirely good.

The company has witnessed vicissitudes in time gone by, but the shareholders have every reason to be satisfied with the success of recent years, and they are justified in looking to the future with some degree of confidence and pleasure. During the year under review raw materials and labour, and latterly pig iron values, have increased in price until, as stated in the report, all have long since become excessive, but in the result, the net profit approaches that usually realised in a year of good trade.

As from 8 November last, the company became a controlled establishment under the Munitions Act of 1915 (which has not been made applicable to iron ore and coal mines or coking plants, whence raw materials are got) and after that date practically four-fifths of any profit which may thereby be realised over the average of the standard years passes to the government.

The Millom and Askam Company have shown considerable enterprise, not only in bringing their plant right up to date, but also in prospecting for ore. Important improvements as foreshadowed in the chairman's speech at the last annual meeting have been carried out at the Millom Ironworks, including the installation of a new water softening and boiler and water cooling plants, as well as the new blowing power, pig lifting and pig breaking and gas cleaning plant.

On this new machinery, close on £40,000 has been expended during the year; while a sum of over £16,000 has been disbursed in connection with the operations at Ullbank, where an extensive deposit was discovered some time ago, and where a pit is being sunk. The progress of this work has unfortunately been retarded by an influx of water, but the contractors are sealing this off by means of concrete. A depth of 310ft has already been sunk, and this enterprise promises to become a successful and profitable one.

The company has 50,000 shares of £1 each in the Whitehaven Colliery Company, where developments have also been in operation with promising results, and £50,000 has been invested in the War Loan. It is altogether a very satisfactory report and balance sheet and complimentary for the board of directors, their able chairman, Mr G. Mure Ritchie, and the whole staff.

Search for New Markets

Making pig iron requires huge amounts of raw materials – coal, iron ore and a limestone flux – and produces mountains of waste slag. The slag still has a proportion of iron in it and various experts laboured over ways to make money from extracting it – usually without success. More exotic schemes were also devised for Millom's waste products including this one described in the Millom News *of Saturday, 3 October 1936, under the headline 'Rubber from Slag'. It said:*

High hopes are being entertained in Millom with the news that an experiment to obtain rubber from slag has proved nearly a success. If this experiment comes to anything the slag banks in the south Cumberland town will provide work for many.

There are millions of tons of slag on the two man-made 'hills' outside the ironworks, which, although being an eyesore, denote the prosperity of the iron manufacturer. It has been stated that the Commissioner for the Special Areas is investigating this experiment, and according to a national paper, some attempts are to be made in other iron centres. The only use made of slag is for road-making. It would be another industry if rubber manufacturing could start in Millom. It would have the backing of many people.

Hammer Blow for Millom

In the mid-1960s Millom Ironworks was looking for a niche market which could keep it alive at a time when the industry was shrinking and surviving plants were getting bigger and bigger. Millom's

Most pig iron and castings left Millom by railway but by the 1960s road transport was playing a larger role and customers expected delivery to the door. The houses of Borwick Rails can be seen in the background.

answer was to promote and develop an experimental process called spray-steel. As the steel industry was nationalised at this time and Millom was, therefore, likely to become a competitor the government of the day didn't go out of its way to help. The money for investment could not be found and Millom Ironworks was doomed – just three years after reaching its centenary. The Evening Mail *of 7 June 1968 broke the grim news. The report said:*

Millom Ironworks is to cease production of pig iron as soon as possible it was officially announced this afternoon. This was stated by the Cranleigh Group of which the Millom firm is a subsidiary.

A special board meeting at Millom Hematite Ore and Iron Company's works was being held this morning, following an announcement in *The Times* that the works was to close. The announcement from Cranleigh said: 'The Millom Hematite Ore and Iron Co. Ltd will cease production of pig iron as soon as practicable. Negotiations are in hand which may lead to the sale of the ore mine, the foundry and other assets. Millom's trading losses during the year to 30 June 1968, have already been indicated to shareholders and so far as Cranleigh Group is concerned a substantial capital loss is inevitable. However, the rest of the group is financially independent of Millom and continues to trade profitably. Excluding the iron and steel division, the group net profit

This 1960s aerial view of Millom Ironworks gives a good impression of how big the site had grown in a century of operation.

Above: *Taking a rest break at Millom Ironworks in the 1960s. Those pictured include Wilf Myers, Jonty Troughton and Slim Kelly.*

Right: *The experimental spray-steel plant at Millom Ironworks in 1965.*

before tax (so far as can at present be foreseen) for the current year ending 30 June 1969, is expected to be approximately £100,000. A detailed circular will be sent to all shareholders within a few days.'

Mr D.R.G. Davies, managing director of the firm, said that the announcement in *The Times* business supplement that his firm has quit the struggle to survive after the government's failure to support the Millom plant's development of spray-steelmaking had been an unofficial leak. Asked if the works are to close Mr Davies said: 'In view of this appearing in *The Times* we feel obliged to say something today.'

The Times states that Millom Hematite will close over the government's spray-steel decision and announces that the closure is likely to happen within three to four months. *The Times* believes that Mr Roy Mason, Minister of Power, was told of the Millom closure decision last week. Millom has suffered from the competition of imported pig iron and the firm's manager has bitterly protested against the government's concessions on imports and the veto on local developments at Millom of the revolutionary spray-steel project which the firm pioneered.

Millom Ironworks employs about 650 and a further 300 in the Florence-Ullcoats Ore Mines at Egremont. The *Evening Mail* has frequently reported the firm's attempts to win government sympathy to its proposed installation of the first commercial spray-steel plant. Gloom, despondency and the forecast of a very bleak winter were the main reactions in Millom today to the news of the closure. The gloom was rooted in the knowledge that little can be done in the immediate future to help the town which will be industrially crippled when the ironworks closes.

Despite firm pressure exerted by Millom Rural District Council and the Millom Chamber of Trade, no positive government action has been forthcoming on the much-wanted advance factory in the town.

The closure of the ironworks comes only months after the closure of Hodbarrow Mine, where 104 men were placed on the books of the Millom Employment Exchange. About 75 per cent of these men have been re-employed. Finding alternative employment for 650 men will be another matter.

Councillor Cyril Porter, chairman of Millom RDC said: 'It will be a bad blow for Millom. The council had been pressing the government for six years for an advance factory for the town.' He added that he would not comment on future council action as it was in recess throughout August.

Mr Harry Partridge, secretary of Millom Chamber of Trade, said: 'As far as the traders are concerned it will certainly hit them very hard. They have not been doing well lately. The industrial scene has been depressed for a while.' He added: 'It looks as though we are in for a very bleak winter.' He prophesied a possible emigration from the town, a move that would hit the 100 traders even harder. The Chamber of Trade had been pressing for a Duddon barrage. 'This would have at least assured that Millom would remain a dormitory town,' he added.

Mr J.B. Symonds, Labour MP for the Whitehaven Division, which includes Millom, said it would be a tragedy if the ironworks was closed. However, he added, he had not been told that the works was to close. 'I feel certain that the Board of Trade would have advised me immediately,' he told the *Evening Mail* from his Jarrow home. Mr Symonds was reluctant to comment further without hearing anything official, though he did add that he would begin making inquiries into the matter today.

The Final Day

The last full day of production at Millom Ironworks saw the town in a dark mood. A parade was held along Devonshire Road which was a combination of a protest march and a grudging acknowledgement that an important part of the town's life had ended. The Evening Mail *of 13 September 1968, summed the day up as 'Black Friday' for Millom's 'lost' 400. The report said:*

More than 400 men working away the final hours of the life of Millom Ironworks were preparing for their Black Friday protest-banner march from the plant gates to Millom town centre this afternoon. The banners they have prepared and a mock coffin are a grim satire on their plight in an isolated town whose male population faces industrial poverty. One slogan spells out the town's name and simultaneously its meaning to the men of the ironworks who are jobless from clocking-off time, 4.30 p.m. It reads: 'Misled, Ignored, Lost, Lied to, Overlooked Men.'

Speeches are still being made in Millom by representatives of the town's organisations and possibly elsewhere. According to some of the ironworks men, however, the time for talk has passed, and government action is now demanded over Millom's desperate need for industries which will be man-powered.

Today, as large sections of the plant are dismantled or trimmed down as negotiable stock, a giant sinter plant which cost about £250,000 and operated at Millom for only a year, stands idle together with a new £150,000 blower which is said to have operated on test only. After shift-work on salvaging and tidying-up the plant equipment yesterday, workers told an *Evening Mail* reporter that their toleration of life on the dole might not last more than a fortnight to three weeks. 'Then the drift out of the town will mount up, and from then on it will snowball,' said Mr Alan Paterson, a fitter, of Silverdale Street, Haverigg. Already Mr Paterson together with two fitters and riggers, Freddie Steel and Tommy McCluskey, have been job-hunting in Scotland – in vain. 'We went to the government's new oil refinery project at Grangemouth, where men were being taken on. But we were told that they only wanted local workers,' said Mr Paterson.

A fitter and turner, Mr George Hockaday, 56, of Market Street, put the case for the older workers. 'We have little, if any, chance of being replaced in this area,' he said, 'and we are in a bad spot to sell our houses and leave. Nobody wants to buy a house in Millom at the moment, so we are stuck here for the time being.'

Councillor Leslie Sawrey, a union convenor at the works, and a Millom representative on Cumberland County Council, agreed that the patience of men on the dole will rapidly peter out. He warned that other factories in the area would suffer when the emigration increases. He stressed the vital need for the Board of Trade to approve a loan to West Coast Tanneries which could ensure the firm's economic security at Millom. Councillor Sawrey protested that authorities in West Cumberland were allegedly using Millom's plight merely to further their own claims for government help to the West Cumberland area.

A letter issued by the Whitehaven Constituency Labour Party to Mr Harold Wilson, Mr Fred Lee and Mr T. Dan Smith, called for new industries at Millom, he said, but it went on to concentrate on the needs for road improvements and a major industry for West Cumberland.

Councillor Sawrey further complained that a Millom crisis deputation to Whitehall next Tuesday was being represented by only one person from Millom, Councillor Cyril Porter, chairman of the RDC. Councillor Sawrey said: 'It is completely wrong that the deputation should comprise the Mayor of Whitehaven, the chairman of Ennerdale Council, Mr Thompson Reed (NUGMW), Mr Joe Symonds MP and Cyril Porter. I feel

A 1960s picture of some of the last miners to work at Hodbarrow.

that Mr Porter's claims for Millom will be overwhelmed by claims for aid to West Cumberland.' Councillor Sawrey said that another public meeting at Millom would be held next Thursday to discuss the success, if any, of the deputation to London.

Defending the government's refusal to take over Millom Ironworks, Mr Albert Booth MP for Barrow states, 'We cannot go on ploughing in money to support a firm which is not commercially viable.' Mr Booth, who was concerned with the business of the Standing Committee of the Nationalisation of the Steel Industry, declared that the plant closure had resulted from a failure of private enterprise.

He said: 'In my opinion, the government were not prepared to use public money to totally underwrite the introduction of spray-steel making into Millom unless the Cranleigh Group was prepared to put money into the enterprise. I am not committing Mr Joe Symonds MP to this view. It is my own. Ideally, spray-steel would have operated much better on a bigger basis than the Cranleigh Group could have put it. The minister would not have objected to the operation of spray-steel on a smaller scale than the maximum because it would have provided jobs.'

The government would underwrite 45 per cent capital support, but the Millom company was seeking more than this. Of the recent claim by Mr D.R.G. Davies, managing director of the company, that the government could have taken over the holding lock, stock and barrel for £1 on condition that the works was kept open. Mr Booth said: 'This meant that the government would have had to take on all the debts and liabilities. In fairness to the government, it has to be said that Cranleigh have had all the advantages that could have been held out to them by the freedom of development area status. Despite that, this privately owned sector of the steel industry has not been operated efficiently to make it a profitable operation.'

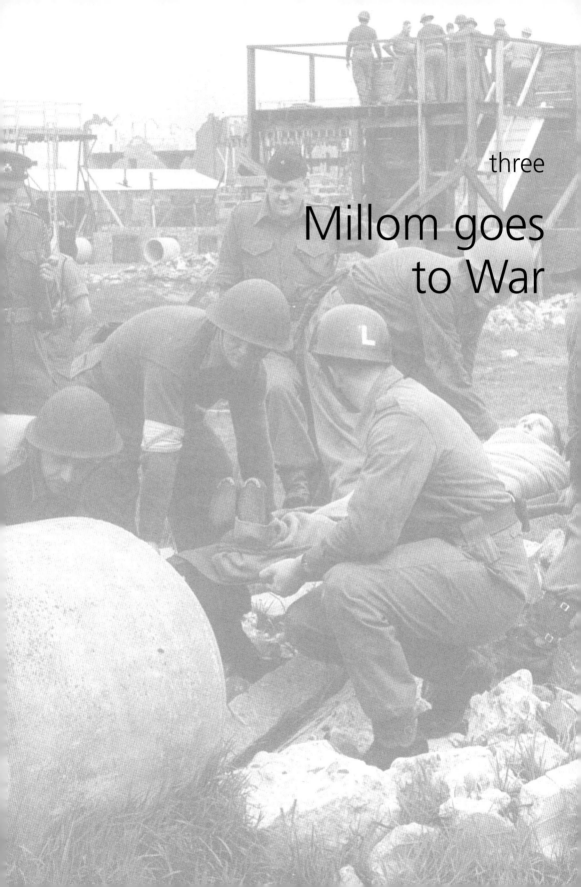

three

Millom goes to War

This picture show the St James Prize Band outside the Tin Chapel on the corner of St George's Road and Mainsgate Road, in 1910. Four years later many of these men would be in uniform as the First World War got under way.

Doing Your Bit

The First World War was the biggest single influence on economic and social change in Millom and Haverigg in the early part of the last century. It killed more than 200 of its young men, took perhaps five times that number for uniformed service and introduced a whole new range of opportunities for women. With so many men serving overseas there was a flood of new jobs for Millom's women – particularly in shops, farm service and in highly-paid but highly dangerous jobs making munitions at Barrow. Special trains were laid on from Millom each morning to take workers to Vickers at Barrow – many of them newcomers to Millom, including more than 1,000 Belgian refugees.

News of the outbreak of a major international conflict started a frenzy of excitement at Millom. It was all seen as a brief adventure not as a long slog set to continue for four years. The Millom Gazette of Friday 7 August, 1914 described the scene under the headline 'Millom Gripped by the War Fever'. It said:

The Millom railway station was crowded with enthusiastic spectators on Sunday morning to witness the departure of the Millom detachment of the 4th Battalion King's Own Regiment for their annual training, which was to take place at Kirkby Lonsdale. The scene presented was indeed a busy one, the men in khaki uniforms working arduously in order to collect baggage, etc. These were trucked all in routine fashion and shortly after 11 o'clock the party, numbering well on towards 100 strong, including commissioned and non-commissioned officers, left Millom for their annual training.

The special editions of the Sunday papers were snapped up with unusual eagerness, and when it became generally known that the war cloud had actually burst, the mothers and wives who possessed sons and husbands serving in the British Army and Navy at once exhibited signs of natural anxiety. A couple of local navy lads on furlough were recalled to their ships on Friday, and this was the first intimation of Britain's attitude displayed locally.

The officer commanding the Millom detachment could give no assurance to the men as to how long they would remain at Kirkby Lonsdale, or even if they would really arrive there. It eventually transpired that the worst was actually to be realised, for the men made their reappearance in town at Monday noon, having been informed that training was cancelled. A number went to work in the afternoon, but on Tuesday morning notices were posted to the effect that men must not go to work, but hold themselves in readiness for mobilization.

The fall-in was sounded at 3.30, and the company under Captain Barratt, paraded at the Jubilee Field. At about 8.15 on Tuesday night a wire was received stating that the Border Regiment were mobilizing at Keswick the day following (Wednesday). It is stated a member of the Border Regiment was in Millom at the time, but was unable to get through until Wednesday morning. In the meantime, the Millom detachment had received orders to meet at 9 a.m. on Wednesday.

Throughout the whole of Tuesday evening the town was in a state of keen excitement, the railway station being besieged by large crowds eager to purchase the latest papers. Some went as far as to pay two pence for an evening paper, but even at this price many were unable to buy. A number of people were observed in the vicinity of the station as late as 11 o'clock, eagerly awaiting the latest news. Our representative was amongst the number, and in answer to a query from a reservist as to whether Britain had actually proclaimed war he was able to answer in the affirmative, whereupon the local reserve, with heart true as steel, remarked that he would at once go home and make ready for an early departure in the morning. He informed our representative that he would be compelled to go to Aldershot.

With the advent of Wednesday, crowds of local residents were early astir, and papers were to be had only at a premium. A couple of dispatch messengers reached Millom in the early hours of Wednesday morning, making eager enquiries for the commanding officer. On returning from his residence they posted the following proclamation: 'Territorial Force. His Majesty the King having been graciously pleased to order by proclamation that directions be given by the Army Council for the embodying of the Territorial Force. All men belonging to the said forces are required to report themselves immediately at their headquarters.'

On the notice board outside the police station a similar copy was posted in addition to the one appended: 'General mobilization of Army Reserve. (Regulars and Reservists). His Majesty the King has been graciously pleased to direct by proclamation that the Army Reserves be called out for permanent service. All regular reservists are required to report themselves at once to their place of joining in accordance with instructions of their identity certificates, for the purpose of joining the army. All special reservists are required to report themselves at such date and at such place as they may be directed to attend for the purpose of joining the army. If they have changed their address since last attendance at drill or training they will report themselves at once by letter to the adjutant of their unit. The necessary instructions as to their joining will be given'.

Shortly after 8 a.m. members fully dressed for marching were seen making their way to the Drill Hall, and by nine o'clock the whole company were in attendance. Mobilization

Millom Territorial Army recruits around the time of the Second World War. From left to right, back row: Bernard Sharp, Jim Nankivell, Basil Jackson, David Foster, Bill Shaw, Don Usher. Middle row: Tom Atkinson, Alan Arnold, Colin Poole, Norris Brown. Front row: Ken Wilson, Norman James, Jack Phillips, Doug Myers, Miles Mason, Alan Pill.

papers were at once handed to each man, and telegrams were received at short intervals, but it was not until about 10 o'clock that the first move was made, when a party, numbering 13, under Sergeant Howarth, entrained for Foxfield, where they will guard the viaduct. About half-an-hour later a couple of men were seen to leave in a motorcar. The men underwent a medical examination during the morning.

The crowd of excited onlookers increased as the morning progressed, but at about 11.30 the company were dismissed with orders to fall in at 12.30, when they would leave for Barrow.

About a dozen men who had served time with the old Volunteer Force and the Territorial Force came forward during the morning and offered their services. They were at once furnished with a kit and now await orders.

Dinner was little thought of by the majority of people, the intense excitement prevailing throughout the early stages of the morning increased tenfold when it was known that the company would leave at 12.30. Trades people, miners and housewives cared or thought little about work, and the vicinity of the Drill Hall was the scene of great enthusiasm, the crowd being eager to give their townsmen a rousing send-off. Inquiries were made as to what time the departure would really be made, and we were informed that 3.38 p.m. was the time fixed, 12.30 having been arranged for the assembly.

Millom, like other places, naturally feels the effect of the war, and whilst there is a tendency for erratic purchasing of foodstuffs, generally the attitude may be considered as little above normal. It is officially stated that orders for sacks of flour etc., cannot be considered, and a leading tradesman received a quotation this morning which announced the fact that sugar had practically doubled in price. Everything will go up, and whilst the firms who supply the town with foodstuffs are prepared to do their utmost in the way of forwarding on supplies, they do not guarantee the carrying out of any order.

From this it will be gathered that extravagant living should be refrained from, and to make the most of everything. At the same time, there is nothing at present to cause undue alarm, and whilst there are ample food supplies in the country to last several months, and there is no reason to apprehend any very serious falling-off in the supplies coming from abroad, there have been panic buying in many quarters. If this goes on there will no doubt be a greater inflation than if people keep their heads and purchase only normal quantities.

Local horse proprietors have this morning been visited by officers desirous of purchasing horses for the government. Mr A.H. Hornby, the renowned cricketer, is reported to have been among the visitors. An inspection of Messrs McNall Bros' stables resulted in the purchase of two horses, which have already been despatched. Mr Glaister's establishment was also visited, and the horses examined, but here there were none for sale.

If rumour is to be relied on, Vickers' are keeping a sharp look-out at Silecroft, and it is reported that a gun has been placed upon the beach. The only official statement forthcoming is that a gun special passed through Millom for trial at Eskmeals this morning.

Promptly at 3.20 p.m. the local company of territorials, numbering 115 strong, paraded to the railway station and entrained for Barrow. Up to the last minute their destiny was uncertain, but prior to the departure of the train a telegram was received stating the men had to proceed to Vickers Ltd.

The crowd of spectators had grown considerably, and hearty cheers were raised as the train steamed out of the station. Fog signals were placed on the line, and altogether the send-off was a very enthusiastic one.

The Home Front

Fears of U-boat attacks, signalling by spies, or even an invasion, prompted the military authorities to put Hodbarrow Outer Barrier off-limits. This ban did not please those in search of fish, rabbits, or a good walk – and some chose to ignore the warning notices.

The first to get caught and brought before Millom Police Court was Robert Proctor, an ironworker of Borwick Rails. The *Carnforth News* of 16 December 1916 reported that he had been challenged by Special Constable Richard Dickinson. The ironworker had been collecting firewood and claimed not to have seen the notices issued under the Defence of the Realm Act. Mr Proctor's case was dismissed as it was the first of its kind seen at the court but he had to pay seven shillings (35p) costs.

The restrictions stopped anyone from approaching within 100 yards of the Outer Barrier – even by boat or walking on the sands when the tide was out! The restrictions were imposed on 21 October 1916 and Hodbarrow watchmen had instructions to report any infringement of the order to the police. They were not lifted until 7 January 1919.

With so many young men called away to fight it was vital to maintain levels of production on the farms both during and immediately after the war when food supplies became short. One solution was the Women's Land Army and the *Millom Gazette* of 17 January 1919 reported: 'Women's Land Army girls working between Broughton and Drigg held efficiency tests at Millom Castle Farm in milking, land work and horse work. Seventeen gained certificates entitling them to higher wages.' In the last few months of the conflict food production was so critical that several Millom soldiers were recalled as farm labourers.

The needs of the army frequently clashed with local employers who were anxious not to lose all their most experienced or highly-skilled staff. Regular military tribunals were held to decide who should go to war and who should stay to maintain Millom's normal services. One example was reported in the *Carnforth News* on 16 December 1916 when Millom Co-operative Society feared the loss of all its branch managers to the army. The Millom tribunal heard evidence that the society had already provided twenty men for the army and another eight for munitions work. The society won a conditional exemption from military service for its Wellington Street branch manager but had to accept losing both its Haverigg branch manager and its Millom bakery manager – responsible for producing 700 loaves of bread a day.

Many from Millom travelled on special workers' trains to Barrow to assist in munitions production at Vickers. The money was good but the hours were long and the work dangerous. Women shell fillers became known as canaries as the chemicals used made their skin turn yellow. At least one Millom man was killed making munitions. Nineteen-year-old George Mason, of Lonsdale Road, died in an accident in the Shell Shop in February 1916.

The *Millom Gazette* of 11 August 1916 reported that Millom munitions worker John Heron worked seven days a week from 7 a.m. to 4 p.m. for £3 5s (£3.25). His rail fare cost 3/6d (17p) a week.

Alongside the Millom munitions workers were many who made the town a temporary lodging place as Barrow was packed to overflowing. In 1916 Millom had shell workers from Portugal and Spain, Belgium, Holland, Switzerland and the Isle of Man.

By the middle of 1918, as victory on the Western Front looked increasingly likely, the food and fuel shortages grew worse in Britain. By November 1918 the Millom Food Control Committee had adopted fifteen members and started work to organise available supplies.

The *Millom Gazette* on 22 November 1918 reported a meeting of the council and said: 'The clerk reported that there were no local supplies of coal in the town, but there were 36 tons on the way, while 200 tons from Whitehaven and 100 tons from Newcastle had been promised.'

Prices rose, particularly for eggs, and people attempted to hoard sugar for jam making. The jam and marmalade ration was fixed at four ounces and you had to hand in a coupon from a special ration book to get it. Restrictions were also placed on lard, sugar, poultry, tobacco, bacon, butter, margarine and tea. Three Millom people were fined twelve shillings (60p) each in October 1917 for bulk-buying sugar. In one case it was 108lbs.

To increase local supplies of food the Cultivation of Lands Order 1916 encouraged councils to create or expand allotments. Millom council advertised five allotments in Mainsgate Road to be cultivated as vegetable gardens in February 1919.

The possibility of Zeppelin raids prompted night-time lighting restrictions in Millom – although no-one ever reported seeing one of the giant airships over Millom. By winter 1916 the restrictions forced many Millom tradesmen to close their shops early at 6 p.m. However the shops remained open until 8 p.m. on Saturdays.

Belgian Parade

At the end of 1914 Millom had a population of well under 10,000 but still managed to squeeze in at least 1,000 Belgians who became refugees from the German military advance. Whole families came and Millom had to find ways to feed and clothe them, find rooms for them to stay and school places for their children. Remarkably all this proved possible and the Belgians played an important role in the life

War brought new job opportunities and more relaxed social rules for Millom's women. Here a group of tennis players are shown in the 1914 to 1918 period.

of the town during the war. They had their own bands and orchestras and even organised parades to mark their national independence day each July. One of these parades was reported in the Ulverston News *of Saturday 28 July 1917. It said:*

Belgian Independence Day was celebrated at Millom on Saturday, when under the auspices of the Belgian Band, a successful carnival was held. The chief feature of the proceedings was the procession, accompanied by five bands. After traversing the principal streets it reached the Market Square where a presentation was made to Mr A. Miller, of Barrow, the Hon. president and founder of the band.

Inspector Huck acted as chief marshal of the procession, which was headed by a motor car, in which sat Mr A. Miller and other friends. The Holborn Hill Brass and Reed Band came next, followed by the Boy Scouts and Trek Carts. The tableau car 'Belge before the War', contained a fine painting by a local Belgian, E. Libon.

After the Belgian children came the Belgian Band in their interesting old peasant costumes. A guard of honour in the old costume of the 1830 revolution was followed by soldiers of the revolution, with an imitation gun. After the Barrow Shipyard Band came the 'Car of Peace', with the war-like declaration 'Down with Germany'. Mr W.H. Woodburn dressed as 'The only lady left'.

The Salvation Army Band preceded the Belgian Society and Aidons les Belges, and groups of members followed by the Haverigg Band. 'Belgium in the War' was a painting which directly contrasted with 'Belgium before the War'. It was the work of another clever local artist L. Lacroix. The tableau car, 'Pour la France', followed, and the procession was concluded with the car 'The Kaiser in Hades', which caused much amusement, the unconscious humorist who decorated the car having placed the Union Jack in the background! The procession terminated in the Market Square, where a large crowd of people had gathered.

Mons. J. Vancraybeck, on behalf of the band, presented to Mr Miller two artistic French bronzes, representing industry and arts, the former being a figure of a forger with anvil and hammer, and 'arts' was represented by the figure of a sculptor. They bore the inscription: 'Homage and gratitude. Presented by the Vickers' Belgian Military Band, of Millom, to its honorary president and founder, Mr A. Miller, 21st July, 1917.'

In making the presentation Mons. Vancraybeck said:

'For the third time we are celebrating our National Independence Day in exile. Excuse us, Mr president, if we say exile, because the Great Albion has done more for us than we ever expected of her. It is not necessary to search the whole of England to find sympathy and generosity. It is sufficient to come to the small piece of land called Millom to find them both together. We shall always remember our arrival at Millom where the population, without exception, gave us a warm welcome. When last year, the idea of having our own band came to a few of us, and having appealed to your generosity to help us with the first expenses you offered spontaneously and loyally to furnish us with the necessary instruments free of charge. You have, Mr president, even gone so far as to help in the inauguration of the band on the 21st July last year.

You can judge for yourself that you have not been deceived in your wishes that is to say that the band has not only played for pleasure but especially to help to relieve our unfortunate population left under the German rule, and for our valiant soldiers who for three years have been defending with glory our dear Belgium'.

Going Home

It was three months after the Armistice in November 1918 before the bulk of Millom's Belgian refugees packed up and headed home. Many of them must have dreaded what they would return to. Their country was free of enemy occupation but scores of villages had been badly damaged or had simply ceased to exist. The Millom Gazette *of Friday, 7 February 1919 recorded the departure of the town's European visitors. It said:*

Above: *A parade by Belgian refugees through the Market Square in Millom on National Independence Day, July 21.*

Right: *The 'Holborn Hill Flyer' from a parade in Millom about the time of the First World War. It is thought to be one of the entries in an event organised by the town's Belgian refugees.*

Opposite above: *This group of Belgian refugees were taking part in July 21 Independence Day celebrations in Millom during the First World War.*

HOLBORN
HILLHI
FLYER.

Practically all the remainder of the Belgian refugees and industrial workers who have formed a colony in Millom during the war left at 8 o'clock on Sunday morning on a special train for Newcastle to embark upon a steamer for transhipment to Antwerp in their native land.

At any one time there were nearly a thousand Belgians, many of them with their wives and families in Millom, but a lot went from time to time to Barrow and other centres, while after the Armistice several went back of their own accord to Belgium, so that their numbers dwindled to about 300.

During the Saturday afternoon the local Belgians removed their belongings to the railway station, every description of vehicle being requisitioned for the purpose, while a great deal of it was borne upon men's shoulders.

The accumulated luggage made a huge stack at the station. About 40 of the male Belgians worked all night pushing up the luggage trucks and loading them, and there was considerable unfavourable comment at the alleged refusal of the local railway authority to provide an engine for the purpose of shunting the trucks into position, thus necessitating the men working all night just before they had to embark on their long and tiring journey home.

The scene upon the platform on the Sunday morning was a memorable one. A large number of English people, amongst whom we noticed three local councillors, Messrs J. Waye, R.F. Docker, G.E. Sheldon and also a magistrate, Mr F.G. Mills, with other prominent residents, assembled and the scene was one of mingled joy and pathos, for while the Belgians were no doubt anxious to again seek their homes in their own country, they had, during their long and intimate association with Millom, made many friends and acquaintances here, and numbers of those leaving were affected to tears, while kisses were freely bestowed upon English and Belgians alike.

Four of the Belgians, a woman, her two little girls, and her brother-in-law, unfortunately missed the train. The police rang up Mr H.J. Kirby JP at the ironworks, and that gentleman at once offered the use of the ironworks' motorcar to convey the little party to Ulverston or further, in an endeavour to overtake the train at one of its stopping places. Owing, however, to unavoidable delay, this was found impracticable, and the mother and her children travelled in the next train.

Only about a dozen Belgians remained in Millom. About 200 Belgians also left Whitehaven on Sunday, while a great number have also departed from other centres in the country.

A letter of thanks written by Francis Brohee was left at the Millom Gazette *office on behalf of the Millom Belgian community. It was addressed to 'the population of Millom', and read:*

On the point of leaving Millom we consider it our duty to thank you for the tokens of kindness that you have shown towards us during these four years of exile which we have passed in your midst.

We shall never forget the sympathetic reception and those tokens of kindness and solicitude by which we have been surrounded during these four years. All through the difficult time of rationing, several among you must have been deprived in order to supply us with the necessaries of life, and so relieve our sufferings in exile.

And very good people it is from the depths of our hearts that we thank you. If a few amongst us have not been entirely agreeable, please excuse them. The misfortunes of war have perhaps affected them more than others. We return to our homes taking the best

This picture gives some idea of the large numbers of Belgian refugees who called Millom their home during the First World War. This is part of a parade through the Market Square.

remembrance of you all. In the name of the Belgians, good people of Millom, please receive our deepest feelings of gratitude and everlasting remembrance.

A Local Hero

As the First World War dragged on and the number of casualties continued to rise, Millom savoured the few chances it had to celebrate success. Perhaps the biggest of these was reserved for the arrival home on leave of Silecroft resident Tom Mayson who was awarded the Victoria Cross.

Tom Fletcher Mayson was born at Silecroft on 3 November in 1893. He was the son of Hodbarrow miner William Mayson. After attending Whicham School and working as a farm labourer he joined the 1/4th Battalion of King's Own Royal (Lancaster) Regiment on 16 November 1914.

The Victoria Cross is Britain's highest award for valour and just over 600 were awarded to the six million people who served during the First World War. In December 1917 a huge crowd greeted Lance-Sergeant Mayson in Millom Market Square and an equally enthusiastic gathering welcomed him at Silecroft.

He told the crowds: 'I am no good at this sort of work but I think it is my duty to thank you all. I am sorry I can't say any more but I thank you all who are present now.'

A public subscription raised more than £200. He was presented with £169 in war loans certificates, a gold watch and an illuminated address recording his bravery

The London Gazette *of 14 September 1917 published the citation to the Victoria Cross award. It was for outstanding conduct during an attack on the German lines at Wieltje in Belgium which began on 31 July 1917. It said:*

For most conspicuous bravery and devotion to duty when with the leading wave of the attack his platoon was held up by machine-gun fire from a flank.

Left: *Silecroft man Tom Mayson who was awarded the Victoria Cross. He was given a big welcome at Millom on his safe return from the trenches.*

Opposite: *The end of war and Britain's major role in world peace was celebrated in Peace or Empire Day celebrations. This Millom group, with plenty of patriotic themes on show, were photographed in around 1920.*

Without waiting for orders, Lance-Sergeant Mayson at once made for the gun, which he put out of action with bombs, wounding four of the team. The remaining three of the team fled, pursued by Lance-Sergeant Mayson to a dug-out into which he followed them, and disposed of them with his bayonet.

Later when clearing up a strong point, this non-commissioned officer again tackled a machine-gun single-handed, killing six of the team. Finally, during an enemy counter-attack, he took charge of an isolated post, and successfully held it till ordered to withdraw as his ammunition was exhausted. He displayed throughout the most remarkable valour and initiative.

Following the war Tom Mayson returned to the Silecroft area, working on the land, as green keeper at Silecroft Golf Club and later at Sellafield. In 1956 he attended the Victoria Cross centenary celebrations held in London.

He died at North Lonsdale Hospital, Barrow, on 21 February 1958, aged sixty-four, and was buried at St Mary's churchyard, Whicham, with full military honours. One of the mourners representing the King's Own was fellow First World War Victoria Cross recipient Harry Christian, who was born at Pennington, near Ulverston.

An End to Conflict

Millom had two major opportunities to celebrate the end of the First World War. The first came with Armistice Day on 11 November 1918. This marked agreement by all sides to stop fighting. It took months of negotiations and treaty drafting before ceasefire officially turned into the Peace Celebrations of July 1919.

There were many informal celebrations for the armistice in Millom, including a free dance hosted by Mr J. Coulson at the Drill Hall and a similar event at the Belgian Club.

In an editorial column the *Millom Gazette* of 15 November 1918 described the bitter-sweet feelings produced by the armistice. It said: 'The glorious news of the ending of the great world war was made known on Monday, and was everywhere received with manifestations of popular rejoicing. There are few homes in the land upon which the war has not laid some cause for abiding grief, but in the thrilling hour of victory our first thoughts and feelings are those of heartfelt thanksgiving that the long agony of blood and tears is over.'

Many felt Millom could have done more to make the armistice a special day. The *Millom Gazette* of 22 November 1918, commented: 'Much surprise was expressed in the town last week that neither Hodbarrow or the ironworks gave their employees a day or two's holiday to celebrate the armistice.' It continued: 'Both at Barrow and Eskmeals, Messrs Vickers Ltd thought the occasion one which their work people could worthily celebrate by a little release from their daily grind. They paid the workpeople during the holiday also. The Millom tradesmen, speaking generally, also behaved very miserly to the people in their employ. They might have realised that it was a case for national rejoicing. Presumably they were afraid of losing a bob or two in their tills.'

For some people in Millom the end of fighting was not followed quickly enough by a lifting of restrictions on the most popular means of celebrating – alcohol. Millom was an important provider of labour for Barrow's shell shops and so shared in the tough rules imposed on drink sales to ensure the workforce remained sober. A Letter by Spartacus to the *Millom Gazette* of 29 November 1918 said: 'The Liquor Control Board, which knows what is good for us so much better than we know ourselves, would like to establish a permanent right to interfere with our private lives, with the wisdom shown in prohibiting a man from paying for his wife's refreshment, and is anxious to continue fostering discontent amongst working men by forbidding them liquor and social relaxation in the only hours they are at liberty, and by compelling them to drink nauseous and watery compounds instead of the beverages they prefer. A war, however,

which has ended in the vindication of democracy and freedom, ought surely to leave behind it a better heritage than a social system based on bureaucratic regulation.'

A Peace Celebration Special Committee was formed by Millom Urban District Council in January 1919 to plan ahead for a series of major town events in July. A Great Joy ball was held in the Palace Cinema, Millom, with tickets at 1/6d (7p) and dancing to a full orchestra between 10.30 p.m. and 6 a.m.

At The Green, a sports day was held in the field of the Punch Bowl Hotel where the wrestling competition was won by Military Medal recipient QMS W. Newton, of Ruskin Mount.

The main Peace Celebrations for the following day were described in the *Millom Gazette* of 19 July 1919. The report said:

'The general thanksgiving and rejoicings in Millom on Saturday will commence at ten o'clock in the morning with a grand procession of the united bands and townspeople.

The place of assembly is the Jubilee Field and the procession will be composed of the police, headed by the Holborn Hill Band, members and officials of the urban district council, education authority, guardians, Millom Fire Brigade, tradesmen's association, tradesmen and inhabitants, Whitwell Lodge of Freemasons and Millom Castle Lodge of Mechanics Friendly Society.

The Salvation Army Band will be followed by the Rising Star Lodge of Mechanics, ambulance corps, Loyal Duddon Lodge of Oddfellows, Sheffield United Order of Druids, Boy Scouts etc. At 12 noon there is to be a united services dinner and at 1 p.m. the children and teachers of the various Sunday schools will assemble in the Jubilee Field and unite in singing the National Anthem, the Old Hundredth and Rule Britannia. Then will follow a procession of the various Sunday schools and included will be the May Queen's car.'

Also planned was a tea for children, sports and games at the Jubilee Field, dancing troupe exhibitions, concert and a fancy-dress contest.

Time to Celebrate

The news that the fighting was over was greeted with delight in Millom although for many it was tinged with the sadness that loved ones would not be coming home. Millom's reaction to the Armistice Day of 11 November 1918 was described in the Millom Gazette *on Friday 15 November under the headline 'Millom Rejoices'. It said:*

The great and welcome news that Germany had concluded an armistice caused, as elsewhere, on Monday, a deep satisfaction in this town. Fairly early in the forenoon groups of people assembled outside the post office and eagerly pressed forward to read a telegram in the window, but it proved, however, to be Sunday's war news, thoughtfully allowed to linger there so that the people's time should not be altogether wasted.

Rumours were current in the town before nine o'clock that the armistice had been signed at 5 a.m., but no official news came through. The first definite confirmation of the fact appeared to come through Mr Ware, the Furness stationmaster, who got the intelligence from the railway authorities.

Then Millom burst with one accord into a display of bunting, flags shot through windows everywhere, and lines of streamers were soon hung across the streets, the market hall clock struck twelve strokes at noon after years of silence, and St George's church bell did its best to become a whole peal. Everywhere delighted faces were to be seen, and by general consent everybody who could turned out into the streets to utter congratulations to each other on the event so eagerly looked forward to.

A joyous procession of Vickers' employees, who had promptly obtained a holiday, came pouring out of the railway station, the girls with their breasts bedecked with small Union Jacks and the national colours, linking arms with each other and with male companions, sang their way homeward, many of them dancing as well.

The Belgium Band assembled with great promptitude and gratified the inhabitants by parading the town, headed by their flag and playing the strains of victory until they must have been exhausted, while a procession formed behind them.

The Millom bands, however, strangely enough, did not, or could not, turn out and it transpired that work was carried on as usual at Hodbarrow and the ironworks, though many of the employees at both places 'took' a holiday on the Tuesday, when the Belgian Band, with a bannerette inscribed 'Belgium Independence, 1830-1918' again did its best to render the occasion a memorable one in Millom.

A Relic of War

Towns competed with each other after the war for the biggest and best military souvenirs to help cement their civic pride and represent their contribution to the war effort. Everything from machine guns to massive field guns were being offered as town and village monuments but what everyone wanted was a tank. Millom was fortunate and its tank lumbered into town at a slow walking pace, as reported in the Millom Gazette *of 27 February 1920, under the headline 'Millom's Souvenir Tank'. The report said:*

Millom let its hair down in August 1945 to celebrate VJ, or Victory over Japan Day. The parade has passed through Millom Market Square and is heading towards the library.

The chief of the war relics which are likely to come to the town arrived on Monday last by rail, and proved to be a very fine specimen of the deadly tank machinery used to such a large extent in operations against 'Jerry' and his ilk in the Great War.

Formerly on active service with G Battalion, the monster is categorised as a Mark 4 female tank (a 26-ton affair) fitted with a 105hp Daimler 'Silent Knight' engine; under active service conditions it would be manned by an officer, NCO and six men.

The work connected with its removal from the goods station to the new Recreation Ground and Park under construction was performed in an eminently creditable manner on Wednesday morning, under the judicious guidance of Lieutenant Meek (Cambridge Regiment, attached to the Tank Corps), and the careful driving of an experienced warrior – Sergeant Prentice, of the Tank Corps – assisted by Privates King, Alexander and Joy.

Considerable excitement was manifest when the cumbersome creation was got under way and driven up Lancashire Road, through the Market Square and so to the Jubilee Field, its evolutions and gambols being a source of wonder to many of the townspeople hitherto unacquainted with the antics of such prodigious mechanical devices; the mud-stained relic was skilfully guided to its last place of honour – a bed of concrete, situate from the Bank of Liverpool and the allotments adjoining the Temperance Hall.

Its final journey performed, a historic snap was taken by Mr S.G. Lamb prior to the removal of the sprocket wheels by the military party.

Previously to the tank leaving the station yard, two live shells – one high explosive and one gas shell – were discovered in the interior and disposed of; the guns had been removed before the tank was despatched to Millom.

The military party engaged in the work connected with the establishment of the tank on its final abiding place were similarly engaged recently at Cockermouth and on Wednesday afternoon proceeded to Whitehaven to further perform duties of a like nature. Sergeant Prentice, it may be stated, has actually been 'over the top' in the Millom tank, which however, only recently came from abroad, and was unloaded at Richborough, the mystery port.

Lieutenant Meek, in charge of the military party, incidentally represented the National Savings Committee, London, who have presented the town with the tank 'in recognition of the nation's gratitude for the assistance afforded in the War Loans by the locality during the war.

Act of Remembrance

Millom has a number of war memorials but only one which represents the entire town. The bells at St George's church were installed as a war memorial and there were many suggestions for other useful reminders of Millom's sacrifice in the war – including a hospital.

On Sunday 24 May 1925, Millom unveiled its new war memorial on a site facing the railway station. The First World War had been over for almost seven years but raising the money needed for the tall column topped by a statue of St Michael had been a struggle for a town hit by recession.

The hard times had struck almost as soon as the fighting finished. The worst effects were on the iron industry which supplied the raw materials for ships and shells – and Millom was a town dominated by iron mining and iron smelting. Many of the survivors of battle who gathered to watch the unveiling ceremony had returned not to a home fit for heroes but to unemployment.

Appropriately the ceremony was performed by a Millom old boy. Major-General Sir Louis Vaughan's father Cedric had been a major player in the development of the town's iron industry.

The *Evening Mail* of Monday 25 May recorded his speech to Millom people. He said: 'When hostilities broke out in 1914 the men of Millom were amongst the first to respond to the call. Many of them took part in the deadly fighting which continued overseas for four-and-a-half years. Some came back – others could never return.'

He added: 'These men who died expected something more than we should raise memorials to their gallantry. They died in the hope we might complete the task in doing which they had lost their lives. That task is not complete. Some people thought that when peace was declared prosperity and plenty would follow immediately. History concerning previous wars proved that prosperity does not come for a long time after war.'

The architect for Millom's war memorial was Mr D. Brundritt, of Ulverston. It was built by Fairbairn and Hull of Barrow and the carving work was completed by Mr A. Miller of Campden.

The *Evening Mail* gave a detailed description of the symbolism behind the memorial's design. The report said:

'The central feature of the Millom war memorial is the statue of St Michael overcoming a dragon – the accepted symbolic representation of the overthrowing of the powers of evil.

St Michael is in armour, and is distinguished from St George by wings, which show that he is not a human saint, but is one of the Archangelic hosts. The spear with which he is killing the dragon of evil is also a cross, typifying the power of the sacred Christian emblem.

On the three buttresses which support the shaft are represented the three main services engaged in the war, and in which the men died who are commemorated in this memorial. These are the soldier, the sailor and the airman.

'The soldier is shown in his long coat representing all regiments of foot soldiers, and the shield over him is the cross of St George, the patron saint of all soldiers (and the emblem of the hospital service).

The sailor is shown in oilskins, and this is not only representative of the navy, but of all sea service. Over him is the ship, the shield of St Nicholas, the patron saint of all sailors.

The watching airman is representative of the defence from the air, and over him are the wings which symbolise flight, and the wreath won for his conquest over the air.

The names of the fallen are cut on the blocks between the buttresses. The shields on the capital are those of Millom; County of Cumberland; the bugle of the foot soldiers and an emblem of the call to war; the anchor, the emblem of the navy.'

An official unveiling ceremony followed a large procession through the town, including children from a number of Sunday schools and bands. The ceremony was described as: 'The actual unveiling of the memorial was simple but impressive. Major-General Sir Louis Vaughan stepped forward, a few turns of the hand, and the flag which had covered the monument fluttered down, leaving the stone revealed for the first time.

A beautiful wreath of laurels and poppies from the Millom branch of the British Legion was placed at the base by Miss Elisabeth Fisher, Master Frederick Sage (children of deceased soldiers), Messrs Thomas Coward and Edward Rodgers (discharged ex-servicemen), and a few minutes later, numerous other wreaths were laid on the memorial, amongst them being one from the officers, warrant officers, NCOs and men of the 4th King's Own Royal Regt (Lancaster), D Company; others from the Millom Urban

Above left: *This is one of Millom's many memorials to the casualties of the First World War. This one is at Holy Trinity church and records the names of forty-eight parishioners.*

Above right: *The unveiling ceremony for Millom's war memorial in 1925.*

District Council, Millom joint education committee, and the members of the Millom sub-division police, with a very large number from the various relatives of the fallen.

Perhaps the most impressive part of the whole ceremony was the two-minutes' silence, at the end of which the memorial was dedicated by the Bishop of Barrow with these words: 'To the glory of God, who has at all times raised up valiant hearts to accomplish His purposes and to the undying memory of these brave men who, fully convinced of the righteousness of their cause, laid down their lives for us, we dedicate this memorial in the name of the Father, and of the Son, and of the Holy Ghost. Amen.'

Cruel Irony

The flu epidemic of 1918 and 1919 is Millom's forgotten tragedy. It killed without regard of age or social standing and unlike most infectious diseases it picked out the young and the strong.

Millom babies, toddlers and teenagers fell victim to what quickly became accepted as an international pandemic. It even killed former Millom soldiers who must have thought they were immune to anything after surviving the horrors of the trenches. At some Millom funerals it was a struggle to find enough fit relatives to carry the coffin and newspapers carried list of relatives unable to attend as they lay sick at home.

Exact figures of flu deaths for Millom will perhaps never be known but certainly by February 1919 Dr Morison, the county medical officer of health, claimed there had been 574 flu-related deaths in Cumberland. There was no wonder cure and medical experts seemed powerless to help.

Dr Morison's suggestion was for local authorities to buy and distribute gauze masks. On a more practical level the medical officer had already banned children from attending places or events where flu was most likely to spread. The *Millom Gazette* of 29 November 1918, reported: 'The county medical officer has issued an order through the Cumberland education committee that during the period that the schools are closed owing to the epidemic of influenza, the schoolchildren are not permitted to attend places of public entertainment, public meetings or gatherings.'

The cause and spread of what was called 'Spanish influenza' was little understood in 1918 but recent research has linked it to the close proximity of young soldiers and diseases in the chickens and pigs which were kept to feed them on huge military camps in France.

As this was an international health disaster it also claimed the lives of Millom people living abroad. They included Albert Cox who had emigrated to Rossland, British Columbia, six months before his death in October 1918. He was the youngest son of George Cox, of Mainsgate Road, Millom. Another to die abroad was George Michell, son of Thomas Michell, of Crown Street. The forty-three-year-old former Hodbarrow miner had emigrated to Perth, Australia, in around 1901.

Millom police officers were hit so badly that an inspector had to be drafted in from Whitehaven. In Haverigg, a forty-two-year-old Hodbarrow miner died, his wife lay ill in bed – and there were eight children to be cared for.

The illness seems to have taken around a week to claim its victims. It made its first appearance in summer 1918 and then returned stronger than ever towards the end of the year and into 1919.

The *Millom Gazette* of 1 November 1918, recorded: 'There are several factors regarding the present influenza epidemic which makes it more serious than the outbreak in July and August. For one thing winter is coming on, and will this year find the majority of people less able to resist attacks from the microbes of influenza, bronchitis and pneumonia, owing to the shortage of fuel, as well as fuel foods, especially fats and sugar and a deficiency of warm woollen clothing.'

The health problems continued well into the New Year and the *Millom Gazette* of 21 February 1919, said: 'Influenza is very prevalent in the Millom district at present, and the local medical men are again having a busy and trying time in coping with the outbreak. The disease appears to be especially rife at Haverigg, whole families being stated to be affected, while many Millom residents are afflicted by it. At the Millom railway station, five members of the staff, including the stationmaster, Mr T. Ware, are off duty, owing to the epidemic. The chairman of the Millom Urban District Council (Mr H.J. Kirby JP) is amongst the sufferers and was unable to attend the council meeting this week, while influenza is also affecting many of the members of the teaching staffs of the local schools.'

From Peace to War

The Second World War from 1939 to 1945 affected Millom and Haverigg in many different ways. There was always the possibility of air raids but for the most part Barrow provided a bigger and more important target.

A water tender bought by Millom Rural District Council around the time of the Second World War.

There was only one raid resulting in loss of life and that came at the Hodbarrow Mines village of Steel Green on 2 January 1941. Wartime censorship prevented the *North Western Evening Mail* from identifying the location of the raid for fear of letting the German authorities know how accurate – or otherwise – they had been.

It is highly unlikely that Steel Green was the target for the German raid but that was no consolation for the families of the five who died.

The *Evening Mail* report, printed the same day as the attack, was headlined 'Bombs dropped on North-West village. Five persons killed'.

It published a brief announcement cleared by London. It said: 'Enemy aircraft flew over the North-West of England early this morning and dropped bombs in one village. Three cottages were destroyed and five persons killed.'

The Millom area was felt sufficiently safe for it to receive a number of evacuee children from industrial towns and cities which were thought likely to suffer badly from bombing raids. Millom and Haverigg people also had to live with the blackout rules, rationing and restrictions on movement. The Home Guard and air-raid wardens became regular sights.

Many men and women were called up for military service and took part in major battles such as Dunkirk and the D-Day landings in Normandy, or were posted to North Africa, Italy or Burma. By the end of the war there were fifty-three names to add to the Millom war memorial.

Millom's iron ore and pig iron played a valuable role in the country's war effort but perhaps the area's most significant contribution was made at Haverigg airfield – known as RAF Millom. Today the site is a wind farm, farmland and a prison but some of the former RAF buildings house a museum with a remarkable collection of photographs and memorabilia from the days when Haverigg turned out hundreds of trained men ready to take their places as flight crew.

The airfield was a busy place in wartime with up to forty aircraft in use. Beyond the runways was a rifle range and moving target ranges.

Learning to navigate a 1940s bomber was a dangerous business and the beaches and fells surrounding Haverigg regularly became crash sites. The first accident appears to be on 8 March in 1941 when a Botha Mk1 crashed and burned out. A week later there was a mid-air collision but remarkably both aircraft – a Botha Mk1 and a Battle Mk1 – managed to make crash-landings at Haverigg. Another mishap came on 15 August 1941 when another Botha Mk1 crashed into the sea and sank two miles from the airfield. Fortunately its crew of two were saved.

One of the most unusual of the uses made of the Haverigg complex was for Civil Defence. It was transformed into Doomtown to give people an opportunity to train in skills needed to deal with an urban housing area wrecked by a major enemy attack.

During 1954 more than £300,000 was spent on a refurbishment project despite there being no clear future use for the site. A statement by Under Secretary of State for Air George Ward was reported in the *North Western Evening Mail* on 8 April 1954. It said: 'Mr George Ward, in a written reply, stated that £317,000 was spent on reconditioning this training establishment. Owing to changes in the rearmament programmes it was no longer needed for this purpose and the ministry was considering whether it should be put to some other Royal Air Force use or close down.'

Planning for Conflict

The First World War was widely known as the war to end all wars. This was the only way the huge loss of life could be justified to the British population. Twenty years later the country was at war again and this time you did not need to be in uniform to be on the front line. As early as 1936 plans were being drawn up in Millom to cope with the effects of attack by air. People hoped for peace but got ready for war. The Millom News *of Saturday, 19 September 1936, described how the town was being slowly prepared for the dangers ahead. The report said:*

Terry Murphy at Haverigg aerodrome pictured with an example of the type of aircraft used for training crews during the Second World War.

The Air Raid Precautions Committee of the Millom Parish Council have already gone into the question of defence of the district.

At a recent meeting it was revealed that on the question of air-raid defences and precautions for the Millom rural area, the county council had written intimating that nothing had as yet been definitely arranged, although the clerk had pointed out the peculiar position of Millom, being so close to Barrow, in case any hostilities should break out and the town be thereby unprotected.

On considering the blacking out of electricity and gas services it was decided that the council be recommended to issue instructions that in case of an air raid the respective managers of all these departments within the rural district be instructed to cut off all lighting within their jurisdiction at a given signal. All windows and lights etc. to be blacked out at the same time.

Buildings and shelters – Mr Holmes (St John Ambulance Association) drew attention to the want of adequate buildings for the reception of casualties etc., which appeared to be negligible at the moment. He also stressed the question of the provision of shelters, particularly for the younger element of the population.

The anti-gas training was discussed and the recommendations of the government department duly considered. The medical officer pointed out the necessity of training in this respect, particularly as regards the public generally.

The committee were of the opinion the police, St John Ambulance Association and fire brigade members should be trained in this respect at the government's expense, and the clerk was instructed to write to the Cumberland County Council with a view to the provision of the necessary materials for this object to be attained.

There being only one fire brigade within the rural area, that at Millom, the question of the council taking steps to ascertain whether the various parish councils within the

Above: *The Rocks at Hodbarrow remain a popular place for summer bathers. It was in this area that the first intensive search for iron ore was carried out. It was strictly off-limits during the First World War.*

Opposite left: *A Civil Defence exercise is under way at Doomtown on the old Haverigg airfield complex, in around 1960.*

Opposite right: *A volunteer casualty is helped down from a wooden structure designed to represent buildings after an enemy attack at Doomtown, on the old Haverigg airfield complex in around 1960.*

rural district of Millom would not be willing to form local volunteer fire brigades for their own localities and act in co-operation with this committee should occasion arise was discussed, and eventually it was decided to take no action at the moment, but that this subject matter to be reconsidered at a later meeting.

At the meeting were Councillors Southward (chairman), Mr Postlethwaite, Mr Cowsill, Mr A. Lawrence (clerk), Mr T. Rich (gas manager), Mr T. Penman (electrical engineer), G.W. Wright (police inspector), Dr I.S. Jones (medical officer), J. Hankey (sanitary inspector), W.B. Miles (captain, fire brigade), J.H. Holmes (ambulance brigade), J. Rich (cadet officer).

Volunteers Needed

As the clock ticked down towards the start of the Second World War there was a call put out in Millom for volunteers to act as air-raid precautions wardens and townsfolk were poised to be trained in the use of gas masks. The Millom News *of 1 October 1938, reported:*

At the monthly meeting of the Millom Rural District Council on Wednesday, Mr J.H. Knox, County Councillor, chief air-raid warden for Millom, made an appeal for more volunteers to assist in the most necessary work.

Mr Knox said the local Air Raid Precautions Committee had been very hard at work making the necessary arrangements for the protection of the people should hostilities break out.

The gas masks had not yet been delivered, although he understood them to be in Middlesex. They should be dispatched to Millom as soon as possible. The committee had made arrangements for distributing the masks as soon as they were delivered.

Birkett (Bert) Moore of Hallthwaites, Millom, in a pilot's uniform during the First World War. He wove blankets at the family's woollen mill and his brother was photographer Harry Moore.

Invalids or aged persons would have their masks fitted at their homes. All polling booths would be utilised for the distribution of the masks.

'I am sorry to say,' went on Mr Knox, 'that we have only 117 volunteers and the enrolment of as many more as possible is urgently wanted. The masks will want assembling when they arrive. That will be voluntary work for over 100 persons.' Major W. Donald Barratt said: 'some places have received their masks already assembled.' Councillor N.J. Rich: 'We have been informed that the masks for Millom will want assembling. We got that from the Carlisle headquarters.'

Councillor J.H. Jenkinson supported Councillor Knox's appeal for volunteers. Out of the 117 already enrolled, more than half were wardens. People were wanted for demolition parties, rescue parties and first aid. 'We are doing all we can,' he said, 'but we want more helpers.'

Councillor Knox said Whitehaven had not received their masks either. The fault lay 'up North.'

In reply to Councillor Jenkinson, the chairman Councillor I.J. Postlethwaite, JP, said the government would pay 75 per cent of the money spent by the council on all air raid precautions work.

Mr T. Penman, the electrical engineer, drew attention to a notice from the Home Office regarding the 'blacking out' of all street lighting in the event of hostilities. Mr Penman said all lighting could be extinguished in a few seconds.

In reply to Major C.E. Dardier, the engineer said the instructions were 'on outbreak of hostilities all street lighting to become non-operative.

four

Town and Country Life

Holborn
Hill Boys
No 5

Above: *A view over the tree tops towards Millom Market Square, taken from the tower of St George's church in around 1920.*

Right: *The Revd Cyril Norman Darrall, vicar of St George's, Millom, and St Luke's, Haverigg, from May 1951. He had been vicar at St John's, Ladywood, in Birmingham and succeeded Canon H. Betts at Millom.*

Going to Church

As Millom grew there was a demand for places of worship to reflect the amazing cross-section of people who had poured into the iron-rich district. Church of England, Non-Conformist and Roman Catholic all sought out temporary places or started raising money to build churches or chapels. Bulmer's History and Directory of Cumberland, *published in 1901, gives a taste of what had been achieved in Millom within forty years of the first houses being built for ironworkers. It said:*

The great increase in the population, consequent on the erection of the blast furnaces, rendered more church accommodation necessary. A new church, St George's, with a separate ecclesiastical district, was determined upon, and towards this object the proprietors of the Millom Ironworks contributed the munificent sum of £7,186.

The plans were prepared by Messrs Paley and Austin, of Lancaster, and the building was completed in 1877. The church is nearly cruciform in shape, and in the Early English style. The aisle is separated from the nave by five large bays, resting on octagonal pillars.

The east window is a handsome one of five lights, representing the Crucifixion, with

St George and St Michael at either side. The church stands on an eminence near the Market Square, the gently sloping ground surrounding it being used as a cemetery.

The benefice is worth £300 a year, with parsonage, and is in the gift of five trustees, and held by the Revd A.E. Joscelyne, Doctor of Divinity. The total cost of the church and residence was between £10,000 and £11,000. The parish room, called St George's Hall, is situated in Lapstone Road. It is used as a Sunday school, gymnasium, etc.

The Catholic church, erected in 1888 at a cost of £1,600, is dedicated to Our Lady and St James, and is built of the hard flinty stone of the Lake District, with dressings of Furness Abbey stone. It is a plain substantial building, consisting of sanctuary and nave, with two vestries. The east window is of stained glass, circular in form, representing the Holy Trinity.

The old church, erected in 1868, has been converted into a school. Adjoining it, and close to the church, is the presbytery. The Revd William Perrin is in charge of the mission.

The Primitive Methodist Chapel, Holborn Hill, is a substantial stone building, erected in 1866 at a cost of, £1,100, and presented to the Connexion by the late Nathaniel Caine, Esq., of Broughton-in-Furness.

The Wesleyan Chapel in Queen Street is a very presentable building, erected in 1872 at a cost of £2,031, and enlarged in 1876 by the addition of a gallery, and again in 1883 by the extension of the building at a cost of £623. An infant school has been added. The chapel will seat about 750 worshippers, and the school, which is well adapted for Sunday school purposes, will accommodate about 650 scholars.

The Baptists and Bible Christians have places of worship in the town. The Baptist church, in Crown Street, is a neat stone building erected in 1884.

Vicar's New Home

One of the ways a town can show its prosperity is through the quality of the buildings provided for its clergymen. The new St George's church had a grand vicarage provided for its vicar. Things were not always so grand and some early vicars of Holy Trinity church had to make do with a tent. The Soulby's Ulverston Advertiser *of Thursday, 18 January 1872, describes the foundation stone-laying ceremony for a new vicarage. It said:*

The old vicarage house stood near the church, and was destroyed in the time of the Rebellion, about 200 years ago. After that time the incumbents of the parish had to dwell in tents until a small house, a mile-and-a-half distant from the parish church was purchased for the living about the year 1790, and since that time has been the residence of the incumbents of the parish.

A new house was very much needed, and the present incumbent has been the means of providing funds for this object. The foundation stone was laid by Mrs Irving, in the presence of a few friends, and a short religious service was performed on the occasion.

Mr Paley, Lancaster, is the architect and Mr Hodgson, Holborn Hill, is the builder. The workmen, to the number of 12, were entertained at a supper in the evening.

Off to School

Another source of local pride was in the building and extension of schools. Millom once had many more schools as different Non-Conformist communities provided their own schoolrooms. Another to have closed is the Holborn Hill School. As government education laws saw the school leaving age

Salvation Army founder General Booth on a visit to Millom. His car is shown outside the vicarage of St George's church, Millom.

gradually rise so better facilities were required. This article from the Millom News *of 19 March 1938, describes how £20,000 was spent to provide Millom with a new secondary school. It had taken fifteen years to get the school built and more than 100 people were present at the ceremony. Parents and guests were given conducted tours of the building by pupils. The report said:*

Millom's £20,000 new county secondary school in Salthouse Road was opened on Monday afternoon by Mrs Sadler of Barrow, whose husband, the late Mr William Findlow Sadler, County Councillor, had worked very hard to make the school an accomplished fact, although he did not live to see his cherished desire materialise.

The first portion of the ceremony was held at the main entrance, while the speeches were delivered in the school gymnasium. Many county councillors, rural and parish council members, education officials, teachers, parents and friends were present, while the school pupils formed a guard of honour.

A most interesting address was given by Professor E.F. Jacob, of the University of Manchester and of Oxford University, while Mr G.B. Brown, director of education for the Cumberland County Council, Major C.A. Vallentine, and others also spoke.

Mr A. Ripley, chairman of the school governors, said it was his honour and privilege to welcome Mrs Sadler and to ask her to declare the building open. They all knew the work her late husband had done, and in the school they had a fitting memorial to his work for the town and the country. It was the Sadler Memorial. He had great pleasure in asking Mrs Sadler to declare the building open.

In untying the silk ribbon, which was stretched across the main entrance, Mrs Sadler thanked Mr Ripley for his kind words about her late husband. She added that it gave her great pleasure to declare the building open and wished success to the headmaster, staff and scholars.

Room for Improvement

By the 1950s the Lapstone Road Boys' School, Millom, was showing its age and needed major repairs. This is how the North West Evening Mail *of 19 January 1954, described the work. It said:*

Extensive repairs to Lapstone Road Boys' School, Millom, have now begun. Last summer dry rot suddenly appeared in the school and two classrooms were closed. The trouble was found to be more widespread than had been thought and after the summer holidays, the whole school was closed and the 280 pupils were scattered in halls throughout the town. Cumberland education committee sent a deputation down to study the position and decided to carry out necessary work.

There was a demand for a completely new school, but this was impossible owing to a secondary modern school being 'on the boards' for the near future. The county architect's department drew up plans and bills of quantities, and the education committee obtained a grant towards the cost, which will be about £15,000. Eventually, the school will be one of the best of its kind in the district.

There will be demolition of a large part of the existing wall and simplification of the roof, which has, at present, varying pitches.

Most important, however, will be the installation of a central heating system which will also serve the infants school.

Heating has always been a bugbear in Millom elementary schools, where, until recently, only stoves were used. These did not prove too satisfactory and in some cases overhead gas heaters have been installed. Central heating will certainly be a big improvement and, added to the other improvements, should make the school as comfortable and pleasant as is possible in the circumstances.

Education for All

Education has always been a political issue capable of splitting public opinion. In the 1950s plans to put a big new secondary school next to Millom's existing grammar school sparked off a protest. Grammar school supporters started a petition to stop the project altogether or to get the new school built elsewhere. The protest failed. The North Western Evening Mail *reported the situation on 25 May 1954. It said:*

Millom Secondary School in Salthouse Road, c. 1940.

Top: *Restoration work on part of the Lapstone Road Boys' School, Millom, in 1954.*

Above: *Pupils at Millom's Lapstone Road School in the early 1960s.*

Opposite: *Pupils at Lapstone Road School in 1925. Included in the picture are Roy Sheldon, Arthur Wilson, Reeny Elwell, Miss Stephens, Mary Tyson, Harry Rowe, Jean Whithycombe, Alan Butcher, Albert Northcoat and George Wollington.*

A score of volunteers are now busy throughout the Millom district canvassing signatures for the protest against the proposal to make Millom Grammar School a 'single' school as is the intention of Cumberland education committee.

It will be recalled that the education committee intends to borrow £97,000 to add a secondary modern annexe to the present grammar school. The official view is that the enlargement of the school, from the present population of 250 to between 700 and 800 will make it more efficient and will attract a better type of teacher.

The objectors believe that the present school should be left alone as it is working well and producing good results and that the education committee should implement its pre-war decision to build a separate secondary modern school on a suitable site, to serve the needs of all the children in the Millom district.

Many signatures were obtained at the recent protest meeting and a campaign of collection has been sporadically proceeding since then, but now a drive has started which will continue for the next eight days.

As well as canvassing Millom, volunteers will petition for signatures throughout the rural district, and forms are already being signed in the villages concerned.

The Revd E.L. Le Poidevin, superintendent Methodist minister at Millom, who has taken the lead in the campaign of protest, said today that householders had displayed an intelligent and informed interest in the petition when approached, and were by no means signing haphazardly, but knew fully the implications of the petition.

'Naturally,' he added. 'I have come up against a number of people who do not agree with our point of view, but these are not in the majority.' (At the protest meeting, out of the estimated audience of 300, only two voted against the resolution to protest to the Minister of Education).

Several hundred signatures have already been obtained but the organisers are confident that they will get many hundreds more, as they feel that Millom parents are deeply interested in the question. After the campaign has concluded, probably in the middle of

Opposite above: *Pupils at Holborn Hill Girls' School, Millom, in 1935.*

Opposite below: *Class 5 at Holborn Hill Boys' School in 1925.*

Left: *A car with its radiator wrapped for cold weather is parked outside the former lakeland Laundry in Lapstone Road, Millom.*

next week, the committee which was formed to organise the opposition to the education committee's proposals will draft a letter to the Minister of Education. The petition urges Miss Florence Horsburgh to, 'have alternative proposals prepared and submitted for your approval.'

Royal Visitor

Royal visits to Millom have always been rare enough to make them special events. Combine a princess with a school opening and you are guaranteed a good crowd. The opening of Millom School by Princess Alexandra – the school hall still bears her name – was eagerly anticipated. On Friday, 30 October 1959, The North Western Evening Mail *described the build-up to the royal visit. It said:*

Next Wednesday will be a day to remember for Michael Gregory, 18, and Margaret Tonkin, 17, head boy and girl at Millom School. For they will be the first to be presented to Princess Alexandra when she arrives at the school on her visit.

Both Michael and Margaret took the advanced level GCE last year and are hoping to enter university next year. They will accompany the princess on her tour of the school and will also have seats on the platform and be at the luncheon. Michael will ask the princess to sign the school log book.

Princess Alexandra will be accompanied by Lady Moyra Hamiliton, lady-in-waiting, and Philip Hay, her private secretary.

The princess is to arrive at Millom by train from Barrow after launching the new liner *Oriana*. After the opening ceremony in the school hall, the princess will be taken on a tour of the school.

The report went on to say:

The princess's tour will take in a gym display, the craft room, wood and metalwork, general science laboratory, library, physics laboratory, technical drawing, commerce,

housecraft and needlework. During the tour they will be met by Mr T. Foster, master of the middle school, and Mr W.T. Gibson, master of the lower school.

Plenty of people were given an opportunity to see the princess during her visit to Millom. On arrival she was driven over the railway bridge and along Devonshire Road, Newton Street, Queen Street, Lonsdale Road, Lancashire Road, St George's Road and Salthouse Road. After leaving the school she went back to the railway station via Huddleston Road, Holborn Hill, Dumb Lane, Queen's Park, Moor Road and Horn Hill.

Bigger Village School

Education in Haverigg has gradually been reorganised to concentrate it on a site off Main Street. The News Series *of Friday, 3 October 1969, described the latest stage as a new extension was opened. It said:*

The official opening of the Haverigg Primary and Junior School Annexe took place on 26 September. Approximately 300 visitors were given an opportunity of looking around this new conversion which has cost £32,470.

Tea and refreshments were served whilst Mr J.H. Bolton, southern area education officer, and Councillor R.M. Singleton, chairman of the southern area education committee, gave short speeches.

The new extension has been in use since May and an open-plan system is now in operation. There are 150 pupils (60 infants and 90 juniors).

Mr J.B. Bowe, the headmaster, has been preparing for the changeover slowly for the past three years, whilst in the old building, so that the changeover has taken place very smoothly. Mr Bowe believes in this new system and has great enthusiasm for it; so apparently have the staff and children.

Mr Bowe says: 'The building is good, the equipment is excellent, but the important thing is the system.' The equipment at the school is never locked up and the children have free access to everything, but Mr Bowe says things rarely disappear, even temporarily, due to the pride which the children, who are responsible for the equipment, take in their work. Children arrive early in the mornings and are reluctant to leave in the afternoons.

Millom now seems to be really ahead in education, the new Catholic School and the new extension at Haverigg will be closely followed with another new school at Moor Road, which is nearing completion and will house Millom infants and juniors.'

Programme of Growth

Buying a house was a novelty until long after the Second World War. Most people rented from a private landlord or sought a council house. Millom council rose to the challenge and turned itself into a major builder. The North Western Evening Mail *of Saturday 5 June 1954, described how this was achieved under the headline 'Rapid Progress'. It said:*

Millom Rural District Council can be proud of its achievements in house building. According to a statement made by Councillor F.G. Wilson, the chairman, in his review of the past year, the council has built, either directly or indirectly, 517 houses in the past 10 years. Of these 244 were erected by the North Eastern Housing Association, and 273 by the council.

A very new Millom School in August 1959, three months before the visit of Princess Alexandra to officially open the building.

The first scheme at Grammerscroft was begun in 1944. Before that there was not a council house in the Millom Rural District. In addition to that fairly considerable figure, about 200 houses have been built by the Ministry of Supply, mainly at Seascale to house atomic scientists.

Despite the provision of these houses, as in every other area, there is still a waiting list of about 300, and the council is not relaxing its efforts. Ninety houses were built last year, and on the carpet at the moment are contracts for twelve flats and four houses at the Millom Settle Street site, twenty houses at Bootle, and plans are being prepared for the building of twelve houses at The Green, which will be the first council houses there, except for two agricultural cottages.

Negotiations are taking place for the acquisition of further sites in Millom, and the council would like to be able to go ahead with a plan for an estate of 100 terraced houses at Devonshire Road. To this, however, (as far as is known at present), the county planning committee has raised an objection in view of the proximity of the slag bank.

As the largest town in the district, Millom has benefited most from the upsurge of house building, but provision has also been made for the outlying areas and there is hardly a parish now where council houses are not established.

For a small authority like Millom, the rapid progress which has been made and which in the space of a few short years has turned the council into the biggest landlord in the area is outstanding. As the chairman said in his review: 'While we have not completely got control of the housing situation, it is certainly improving every week, and we compare extremely favourably with other councils of a similar size'.

Storm-Lashed Shores

The weather was a frequent talking point in newspapers. The first cuckoo or earliest lamb was reported each year. One of the earliest newspaper mentions of Millom was in 1796 when violent storms struck the West Cumberland coast. The Cumberland Paquet *report for 2 February describes what happened. The original spellings have been retained for what would now be Rottington and Borwick Rails. It said:*

This group was captured on film in the 1920s at Haverigg School. It shows Group IV of girls and infants.

In Millom, several fences have been thrown down, particularly about Salthouse, Rottenton, Burrow Craits, Patern-Field etc., but the loss is not great. In many places, they were obliged to turn the cattle out of the cow-houses.

In one part of this lordship, two channels, at a considerable distance from each other, up which the tide flows, were united for the first time; at least there is no tradition of their ever having joined before. The water increased so that it covered more than 40 acres of ground.

An old inhabitant of one of these houses relates that her father, who died several years since at the age of 90, frequently said that the water would never hurt them; for that only once, when he was a boy (in such a flood as had never been known before) the tide came to the threshold of the door. In this memorable storm, the tide was 4ft deep within the house.

A Career Success

Many Millom-born people left the town to follow career opportunities in many different fields. One to do so with success was Mr W.V. Nicholas who became a chief constable of police. His story was told in the North Western Daily Mail *of Monday 13 May 1929. It said:*

Mr W.V. Nicholas, chief constable of Guildford, who was born at Millom in 1870, has just passed away. He leaves five sons and two daughters.

One of his sons is an assistant surveyor at Grimsby, and another is in the police force at Portsmouth. The deceased joined the Burnley borough police on 28 January 1895, and in 1901 was appointed sergeant.

From Burnley he went to Oxford, where he obtained the position of senior inspector and chief clerk, and also inspector of weights and measures. His ambition to obtain the position of head constable – cherished from the time he first put on uniform – was gratified when he was appointed to Guildford in December 1909.

Mr Nicholas was nearly 6ft in height and of fine physique. He possessed a rich and powerful bass voice and was at one time in great demand at concerts. He was a member of the Oxford Lodge of Freemasons and was almoner of the Royal Alfred Lodge at Guildford at the time of his death.

Danger on the Fells

The closeness of Black Combe and the Lakeland fells meant there was always going to be mishaps for walkers, farmers and even aeroplanes from Haverigg or Walney flying into mist and fog. To respond to these types of accident a Millom search and rescue squad was formed from volunteers. Its creation was described in the North West Evening Mail *of 27 April 1954. The report said:*

Millom Search and Rescue Squad came into being at a meeting in the council chamber last night. It was intended to call it a mountain rescue squad until someone pointed out: 'We haven't a mountain in the district.'

Councillor Bickerstaffe, of Millom Parish Council, said the idea of forming such a unit arose from the fruitless police search on Black Combe recently for a missing plane.

He pointed out that there were already rescue squads in the Lake District and at Whitehaven. Millom was the only 'missing link'.

The West Cumberland Hospital management committee would provide equipment – probably all first aid. Other kit would be needed – protective clothing for instance – and it would be one of the duties of a committee to raise funds for this purpose. Any squad which was formed would be under the jurisdiction of the police.

Many local organisations were present at the meeting in the council chamber over which Councillor F. Cooke presided. Answers to questions revealed that the nearest squads to Millom were at Holmrook in the north and Coniston in the east and that although there was little question of the local RAF station joining in operations, an air force rescue team had come from Ingleton on the occasion of the plane search. Councillor Bickerstaffe was appointed secretary of the squad and a committee of 13 was elected.

Off to the Pictures

Millom Palladium, which started life as the Recreation Hall, has always played a prominent role in providing entertainment in the town. This outline of its history is drawn from an interview with Don Myers, of Surrey Street, Millom. He said:

The Millom Recreation Hall, or The Rec, opened in 1910. Millom had grown very quickly with the incoming of miners from all over the British Isles. They formed their own concert parties and choirs. The choirs used to have silk suits and the men wore big, wide pants which fastened at the ankles.

The shows used to be mainly singing then someone would tell a tale and cause a bit of a laugh. They used to make use of a marquee where the Palladium is now. The area was also used as a rugby ground. At that time the cenotaph was Docker's Field where horses were kept to pull carts.

My first recollection of The Rec was when we had a concert for all the children whose parents were unemployed – that meant nearly every child in the town. We were given a tea, a bag and a bottle of pop by Tom Fawcett, whose pop factory was in Holborn Hill. This was during the 1920s when Millom suffered a major slump as First World War orders for iron ore and pig iron dried up. Those that had work tended to be on short time. The mines laid many people off and the ironworks frequently worked one week on and two weeks off.

There used to be great big banks of unsold iron ore. The kitchens at Millom Infant School, known as The Cookery, were used during the 1920s as a soup kitchen. Girls used to go there for half-a-day a week to learn how to cook. We had to take a spoon and a tin plate. I didn't like that at all.

The early Millom Recreation Hall was a multipurpose venue. There used to be cinematograph shows. We used to sit on wooden forms and the men moved them out of the way for dances. You could sit on the wooden tip-up seats for 6d (2p). The plush seats downstairs were 9d (3p) and it was a shilling (5p) or 1/3d (6p) in the upstairs circle.

Music for the dances was from a piano, violin and drums but mainly just a piano. In the early run-up to the Second World War trumpets and saxophones were introduced by Harry Pellymounter. The Rec became the Palladium when it was taken over by a cinema company.

I can remember the talkies coming to Millom and the coloured films. One of the first films in colour was *Rose Marie*. It was often a full house for the films. There were nightly shows at 6 p.m. and 8 p.m. with a Saturday matinee at 2 p.m. The cinema was good at promoting its shows and used big advertisement hoardings near the Railway Bridge, in Lapstone Road and near Mainsgate Road.

Welcome for a Duke

The Duke of Kent visited Millom in 1936 as part of his West Cumberland tour to see projects for the unemployed. The region was suffering from a series of trade recessions stretching back to the First World War. He visited Millom Social Centre in Lonsdale Road, Haverigg Occupational Centre, Cleator Moor and Workington. The Millom News *of Saturday 24 October recorded his progress. It said:*

The name George signed with a journalist's fountain pen heads a list of names in the Millom Social Centre as a permanent record of Monday's visit. The Duke had a vociferous welcome from hundreds of loyal citizens and schoolchildren. Nearly everybody carried a patriotic emblem while the streets were gaily decorated with flags and bunting.

At Duddon Bridge, which marks the boundary between Lancashire and Cumberland, the royal visitor was met by the chief constable of Cumberland and Westmorland, Mr P.T.B. Browne, who accompanied the party to Millom, travelling in the police car which preceded the car in which his Royal Highness was travelling. As the royal car approached the Millom Centre, which is situated at the foot of Lonsdale Road, loud cheering broke out. 'Here he comes' was the sign for hundreds of lusty throats to voice a welcome.

As the Duke stepped from his car, he was introduced by Captain Ash Moody, of Leeds, to Councillor John Newton JP, chairman of the Millom Rural District Council, and to Mr A. Ripley, chairman of the town's committee; Mr J. Stoddart, secretary; Mr J.E. Watson, treasurer and Mr J.H. Knox, chairman of the centre committee who conducted the Duke over the premises.

On going into an upstairs room he was introduced to the other members of the town committee; Messrs W. Fawcett, J. Saunders, J. Taylor, J. Nicholson, W. Dawson and Captain R. Hutton-King.

Millom Palladium was opened as the town's Recreation Hall in around 1910. It has served as a theatre, cinema and bingo hall.

The Duke chatted for a short time with several unemployed men before descending the stairs to other parts of the centre. He inspected an exhibition of work, including chairs and articles of furniture, and watched men at the cobbling class at work. He asked several questions and spoke to each man individually.

As he emerged from the cobbling class he was introduced to Mrs Knox, chairman of the Women's Social Centre (town's committee). Mrs C. Whitfull, secretary, and also shook hands and spoke to Miss Kathleen Fox, who has been blind from birth. Miss Fox takes an interest in the activities of the social centre.

On going into the woodwork department, he was asked by Mr F. Boundy and Mr T. Knuckey to drive a small brass upholstery tack in a plush-covered stool which they were making. The Duke smilingly obliged and spoke a few words to the men.

On completing his exhaustive inspection of this section a presentation took place. Mr Cecil Evans, secretary of the centre and upholstery instructor, said: 'I wish to present, from the members of the Millom Social Centre, this small oak chair for your son, Prince Edward.' Smiling, the Duke replied 'Thank you, very much.' The chair is to be exhibited at the centre before it is forwarded to London.

On the route to Haverigg, Queen Street, Newton Street, School Terrace, St George's Road, Moor Road, Haverigg Road and Poolside were groups of people all cheering, especially the schoolchildren outside the Lapstone Road and Holborn Hill schools.

Home for the Aged

The News Series *on Friday, 15 August 1969, described progress on the building of Millom's new home for the elderly in Lapstone Road. It said:*

An £82,000 showpiece, Millom's first home for the aged, will be ready to receive its first residents at the beginning of September. It was opened for a special press preview yesterday. Commented the matron, Mrs P.D. Fitz: 'It is better than a hotel.'

Lapstone House, situated between Lapstone Road and St George's Road, Millom, will be able to cater for 35 residents, 10 in supported flatlets. The flatlets, both single and double, will enable people to bring their own furniture, carpets and ornaments. Each kitchen has a refrigerator, electric cooker and an abundance of cupboards. The cost of a single flat will be approximately £3 4s a week and of a double £3 7s 5d (this does not include an extra charge for communal heating).

Voice and buzzer communications systems are installed throughout the home and flatlets, and these are linked with the staff accommodation to ensure 24-hour supervision of all occupants at all times. Lapstone House has, as well as the usual communal lounge, a tea bar. This will serve early morning tea at 7.30 a.m. and afternoon tea. The matron said it was hoped the tea bar and the communal lounge would form a focal point between both the home and the people in the flatlets. Although both places were separate, a door linked them.

Lapstone House replaces The Croft, Kirksanton, an adapted building accommodating 19 elderly residents. The residents and staff of The Croft will be the first occupants of Lapstone House. Commented Mrs Fitz: 'At first the people were not looking forward at all to the change but since they have seen the new home they are completely sold on the idea.'

It was at first thought that a bus would have to be hired to transfer the residents of The Croft to Lapstone House, but local people have come forward and offered their cars for the purpose. One official commented: 'This home is the best of its kind in the county'.

Health Provision

Funds are still raised today to buy pieces of expensive medical equipment. Back in 1938 Millom needed a new ambulance and the story of its purchase and presentation ceremony was told in the Millom News *in January. It said:*

Millom's new ambulance, a 25hp Vauxhall fitted with all the latest equipment, was dedicated by the Revd E. Rogers, vicar of St George's, Millom, in the Market Square on Saturday afternoon before a large crowd. The Revd R. Trotter and the Revd E.W. Gibson and Major Aldred (Salvation Army) were present. After a prayer and the dedication, the hymn 'At even 'ere the sun was set' was sung.

Mr A. Cowin, chairman of the ambulance committee, in handing over the new vehicle to Councillor S. Park, chairman of the parish council, said he was really handing it over to the people of Millom and district to whose service it had just been dedicated.

The residents were its rightful owners. The ambulance had been purchased solely by virtue of generous support and the untiring efforts of Mr J. Sleep honorary secretary of the Motor Ambulance Association.

The old ambulance had rendered long and faithful service, but its period of efficiency had come to an end. In parting with the old machine, Mr Cowin emphasised the point that it had never let them down. He hoped the new ambulance would prove as efficient as the old.

Mr Cowin appealed for future support to the good cause, and added the hope that nobody would require the services of the machine. He added 'you never know who may need it next.'

Councillor S. Park, in accepting the new ambulance on behalf of the townsfolk, said it was one of the things they really did need in the town. He congratulated the committee on their untiring efforts to secure the new ambulance which belonged to the townspeople, and to whom they had to look for financial support. He had great pleasure in handing the ambulance back to Mr Cowin on behalf of the working committee.

Millom Old Age Pensioners Association used to select its own queen each year. This picture shows the crowning ceremony for 1958 held at the Tin Chapel on the corner of St George's Road and Mainsgate Road.

Councillor N.J. Rich, treasurer to the committee, said the new ambulance cost £656. The first ambulance, a Ford, was purchased in 1922 at a cost of £473 10s, and the second, an Austin, was purchased five years later at a cost of £615. He thanked the public for past support, and sincerely hoped they would continue in the future. Mrs Cowin then opened the ambulance for inspection and appealed to the public to give freely.

The new ambulance, headed by the Holborn Hill Royal Brass Band and later by the Millom Temperance Band, was driven around the town and also to Haverigg. A house-to-house collection was taken at the same time.

Market a Cash Drain

Millom has been a market town for centuries but by the time of the Second World War the town could no longer make any money from holding a market and the Market Hall, under the Town Hall Clock, was thought to be a drain on the town's finances. The Millom News *on Saturday, 28 March 1942 described its final days. It said:*

Millom's Market House, which has been more or less a white elephant for years and a bone of contention among councillors, is to be closed. It has been obvious for some time that an annual loss of approximately £60 could not be tolerated.

Older townsfolk will remember when the Market House was a busy place with an equally busy scene on the square outside. Councillors have blamed hawking for the decline in markets, but Millom is not alone in this respect.

All over the North West it is the same story. Markets are declining, and in many places market day has become a memory. New days bring new ways and we cannot stand still.

Any Old Iron?

A stroll around the grander terraces and public buildings of Millom reveals low stone walls which still bear the scars from where ornamental iron railings were removed during the Second World War. With

U-boat attacks on convoys and pressing military need for iron and steel it was thought unpatriotic not to offer your railings and gates to the government scrap collectors. In recent years some properties have attempted to replace the railings but often you can just see the ground-down stump where they used to be. The Millom News of Saturday, 28 March 1942, told the story. It said:

The work of removing iron railings goes on apace, but the more seen of it the less it is liked, particularly the manner in which it has been done. In burning off wrought-iron why should pieces be allowed to project an inch or more?

Children have a trick of trailing their hands along walls, and if they come in contact with these sharp stumps there will be some work for doctors or ambulance men.

At least one wooden gate has appeared to replace a removed iron one, and others will no doubt follow if timber is available. People who have lived behind iron railings and gates seem to be diffident about their newly acquired outlook.

Fresh Horizons

From the 1850s onwards the Millom district gained people but by the 1890s, and particularly after 1900, it started losing them. People were much more willing to move to job opportunities in the Victorian and Edwardian age. Many miners read optimistic newspaper articles about gold finds in the United States, Australia or South Africa and simply set off in search of fame and fortune. Most were to be disappointed and were back in Millom a few years later when trade conditions were good. An article from the Millom Gazette on Saturday, 23 July 1892, shows how far Millom and Haverigg people could wander. It said:

Marriage of a former Haveriggian in Mexico – Mr Frank Jenkins, formerly of Haverigg, was recently married to Miss Bella Rowe at Trinity ME church, Calle Gante, Pachuca, Mexico.

The bridegroom is a well-known mining captain of Pachuca, and is justly popular with all who know him. He is in charge of one of the largest mines in the Pachuca district.

Money Matters

To build a new town you need money and the banks and building societies were quick to respond. The section of St George's Road which passes through Millom's Market Square has been the town's financial centre for decades but Holborn Hill village had the district's first banking services. The Barrow Herald of Saturday, 2 February 1867 describes the activities of one of the first financial organisations to spring up. It said:

The annual meeting of the members of the Holborn Hill Building Society was held at Mrs Beethom's, the Station Hotel, Millom, yesterday evening week, and was numerously attended.

Mr Jackson, of The Hill, was called to take the chair, and after a few introductory remarks, called upon the secretary to read the annual report, which was very satisfactory to the society which (although only having been established one year) is paying a divided of between 13 and 14 per cent.

New directors for the ensuing year were appointed, and the accounts passed, after which a further sale of shares took place. A vote of thanks to the chairman and the retiring directors, proposed by Mr W.T. Manclarke, the solicitor to the society, brought the proceedings to a close.

five

Industry and Commerce

In the days of Millom's period of most rapid growth, through the 1860s and 1870s, the sea was a major rival to the railways in transporting goods. The Millom harbour developed trading links throughout the British Isles and quickly became a small but important centre for shipbuilding.

The port and shipbuilding centre of Amlwch in Wales had been associated with the Millom iron ore trade from the earliest years. Amlwch ship-owner and builder William Thomas made the links stronger by opening a shipyard at Millom, in partnership with William Postlethwaite.

The firm of William Thomas & Company began work at Borwick Rails in 1870. It employed around a dozen men led by Hugh Jones, a foreman-shipwright from Amlwch. The first vessel to be built was a 115 ton, two-masted schooner, measuring almost 90ft and called the *Nellie Bywater*. It was ordered for the Duddon Shipping Association.

This ship was launched on 20 December in 1873. The first master was Captain Richard Morgan of Amlwch. Most voyages took iron ore from Millom to South Wales, then coal to Ireland, and back to the Duddon with timber for the Hodbarrow pits.

Nellie Bywater was sold to an Irish firm in 1921 and was requisitioned for war service in 1940. Following the Second World War the ship was sold to Captain Richard England.

He combined traditional cargoes with appearances in films. In 1951 the schooner was due to head for the Caribbean but ran into prolonged foul weather in the English Channel. After six days of gales the ship foundered near Bolt Head, Plymouth, on 28 December. One of Captain England's daughters and a crewman drowned. Nine other crew members were rescued by the ship *Careful*.

An iron ore schooner off Hodbarrow Pier, Millom, c. 1914.

The Emily Barratt, *launched in 1913, is pictured at Millom Pier.*

The second schooner to be built at the Millom yard was the 200-ton *Countess of Lonsdale*. This was a wooden three-masted schooner of 113ft in length and was launched on 27 September in 1878. The first master was Captain Lewis Hughes of Amlwch. In April 1890 the ship was under the command of Captain Robert Roberts and sank in a collision with the steamship *Sherbro*. All the crew members were saved.

The yard then branched out into the construction of steamships, building three for the Lady Kate Steamship Company.

The launch of the 191 ton, three-masted schooner *Greyhound* in 1886 marked the end of an era and was followed by a change of name and ownership at the Millom shipyard.

The *Greyhound* operated from Amlwch and frequently sailed to Spain, Morocco and Brazil. It was sold to South African owners in October 1891 and traded to Mauritius and St Helena. In March 1912 the ship was sold again to an owner in Mauritius but sank after hitting a reef at Raphael Island on 15 June in 1913. The 18 people on board were saved.

Hugh Jones and his brother Micaiah became the new Millom shipyard owners and the firm was known as the Duddon Shipbuilding Company.

The first two ships built at the newly named yard were schooners for the Duddon Shipping Association – the *Florence Petherick* and the *Happy Harry*.

The *Florence Petherick* was a two-masted schooner, launched in July 1890 and costing just over £2,000. It worked in the Duddon-Clyde iron ore trade. The ship was lost in a collision with the steamer *Duke of Lancaster* off Copeland Island on 9 March in 1904 while taking coal from Troon to Bray. Captain John Ellis and the three crew members were rescued.

The *Happy Harry* was a 142 ton, wooden three-masted schooner launched on 5 July in 1894. The ship was sold to Job Tyrell of Arklow in 1921 and had a motor fitted in the early 1930s. It survived much longer than most schooners but was grounded off Southport on 15 September in 1950. It was refloated and was anchored at Southport only to drift into the pier causing extensive damage. The ship was demolished and finally burnt on 19 October. The ship had been named after Harry Arnold, a director of the Hodbarrow Mining Company.

Another fine ship built in the Millom shipyard of Hugh Jones was *Becca and Mary*. It was a barquentine built largely of exotic teak and was just over 160 tons. The ship was launched on 14 July in 1904. In 1913 the ship was sold to owners from Portugal and underwent rebuilds and name changes to *Figueira*, *Alcion* and finally *Louzado*. After a career of almost 50 years, the ship was lost while fishing for cod off the coast of Newfoundland in August 1953.

Duddon Shipbuilding Company's final ship, and perhaps its best known, was the *Emily Barratt*. The two-masted schooner was built for Hodbarrow Mines and was launched on Easter Monday in 1913. The ship was sold in 1922 and provided a floating anchor for a barrage balloon during the Second World War. The *Emily Barratt* continued to trade until 1960 and was then converted to a yacht. The ship was brought to Barrow's Dock Museum for preservation and display but deteriorated to such an extent that it was broken-up in 1999. A sad end for a fine ship.

Perils of Life at Sea

Trading by ship could be a dangerous occupation for the captains and crews of the wooden schooners, steamships and tugs which came in and out of Millom harbour. One of the most prominent accidents resulting in loss of life involved the schooner Coniston, whose final hours were reported in the Ulverston News *of 8 September, 1917. It said:*

The schooner *Coniston* was wrecked on Sunday, off Haverigg. The schooner, which is owned by the Hodbarrow Mining Company, was returning from Ireland with a cargo of timber, and is supposed to have experienced a heavy gale in the Irish Sea.

When she entered the Duddon Channel she was in a helpless condition. Preparations were being made to send help, but when the schooner reached Haverigg about 10 o'clock she suddenly sank and disappeared from view.

A heavy sea was running, and it was the highest tide that has been experienced for a long time. A sharp lookout was kept for the sign of any survivors, but no one was observed.

When the tide had ebbed no sign was found of the schooner, but it was afterwards observed that the tide had carried her up the channel onto a sandbank. Five men put out in a boat, but found the schooner had turned turtle.

The tide left her dry, but efforts to right her proved unavailing, and as darkness was setting in and the tide beginning to flow, the men left her. It was reported that a raft had been seen going from the ship towards Barrow, but the police have been unable to obtain any confirmation of the report.

On board were father, son, and daughter, and an able seaman, their names being as follows: Joseph Dunne, mate of the ship; William Dunne, master; Miss Kathleen Dunne (who was on a holiday trip) and Joseph O'Toole, able seaman.

The newspaper article gave a full account of the inquest which tried to establish what caused the shipwreck. It reported:
Captain Edmondson, master of the Hodbarrow tugboat, gave evidence of identification. He was well-acquainted with the men.

William Dunne, who was 21 or 22 years of age, was master of the *Coniston*, a schooner of about 145 tons; Joseph Dunne, who was over 70 years of age, was the father of the first-named, and acted as mate, and Joseph O'Toole was able seaman. He last saw them alive on 25 June, when he took the boat out and parted from it at the bar buoy of the Duddon Estuary.

The *Coniston* went to Ayre, and afterwards to Bray, near Wicklow, Ireland. Witness was expecting the schooner to return at any time, but on account of bad weather it put into Ramsey. He was kept in touch with the movements of the boat, and afterwards knew that it was endeavouring to get through to Millom.

He did not see the *Coniston* when it came on Sunday morning. It was an old boat, but was well found in every respect, and would withstand any ordinary storm, having been repaired recently.

On Sunday morning a strong wind was blowing from the west and a heavy sea running, but he had seen more sea and had known boats come through all right. The schooner was laden with timber and had a deck cargo.

Reviving the Shipping Trade

Although the glory days of Millom as a port had long past there were still periodic attempts to revive the trade. The Barrow News *of Saturday, 1 September, 1951 reported on one of these experiments under the headline 'Millom to be port again'.*

In 1951 an experiment was tried to revive the coastal shipping trade from Millom. This is the Barrow coaster Ford Fisher *loaded with 400 tons of pig iron bound for Swansea.*

Resuscitation of shipping of pig iron from Millom Ironworks, which was recently restarted after a lapse of 11 years, has been reported to be a success and in future cargoes will be sent every fortnight.

This information was given to the *News* on Monday by Mr J.A. Faull, general manager of the ironworks, who said that a ship – it will be the *Ford Fisher* again – would be calling at the ironworks pier shortly to load more pig iron.

'The experiment was a success from every point of view,' said Mr Faull, 'and we shall be continuing to ship iron out on the spring tides.' He continued: 'Cargoes will be taken by sea to South Wales and after the return visit of the *Ford Fisher*, larger boats will be calling at the pier.'

All the ships will arrive at Millom in ballast. This means the revival of trade from the port of Millom which ended when the war began in 1939. Until then there had been a fairly regular traffic in coastal vessels which loaded pig iron at the ironworks pier for South Wales', Scottish and continental ports.

That trade was the successor of a former large shipping industry, originally carried out by the Hodbarrow schooners, which loaded iron ore from Hodbarrow Mines and brought in coal and pit props. The iron ore, coal and timber trade disappeared some time ago.

Shipping is now done only with spring tides. It is impossible to ship on the neap tides because there is insufficient depth of water.

Tough Times Ahead

As the First World War ended so did the good times for Millom and Haverigg. Shipyard and munitions workers were no longer needed and as demand for iron and steel plummeted, so did trade for Millom Ironworks and Hodbarrow Mines.

The war was followed not by one trade recession but a whole series of them. It resulted in two troubled decades with real prosperity only returning by the mid-1930s when Britain started to get ready for the next world war.

The worst years for Millom in terms of unemployment and social hardship were between 1920 and 1922. Demand for iron was so bad that Hodbarrow Mines stopped production. A partial restart was reported by the Millom News *of 22 July, 1922. It said:*

Some eight companies of miners started work at Hodbarrow on Monday morning. Several other companies are waiting instructions, and the fact that the mines have re-opened has brought the greatest satisfaction to Millom, where everyone is now hopeful that the long period of depression has passed over.

The view is confidently held that Millom will soon regain its old-time prosperity and become once more a town where unemployment is unknown. Now that Hodbarrow has made a start again, it is felt that this view is perfectly justified. The better economic news continued as Millom Ironworks stepped up production – although still at very low levels.

The *Millom News* of 9 September 1922 said:

A second furnace of the Millom and Askam Hematite Company will be put into blast on Monday next if, as is confidently expected, the necessary preparations can be completed. This will be welcome news for Millom ironworkers, who for the past two years have been working only a third of the normal week with two intermittent periods when there has been no work at all.

The company has six furnaces at Millom. Three were kept in blast until 1920, but at the beginning of 1921 all were closed down. One was restarted, and except for a period early in this year, that has continued smelting since.

The *Millom News* of 18 November 1922 outlined attempts by the town's council to create employment. There were plans for three road schemes, including one to link Devonshire Road to Haverigg with a new route across the fields. Councillors heard:

That would not be a big undertaking, but it would employ a larger number of men for a longer time. Many men in the Unemployment Club had been out of work for nearly two years, and there was little prospect of a big and speedy revival of employment.

It was planned to spend £4,800 on improvements to Moor Road through a mortgage with the secretary of the Public Works Loan Commissioners. Millom joint education committee was providing free meals for the children of the unemployed. The *Millom News* of 11 November in 1922 said:

During the last week 284 breakfasts and 721 dinners had been provided at Millom and 109 breakfasts and 319 dinners at Haverigg. There were many less official attempts to help the plight of the Millom and Haverigg families worst hit by trade recession. The Primitive Methodist church schoolroom in Haverigg had its own canteen committee to supply free meals for children.

Millom police station appears to have acted as a distribution point for donations of clothing for children. At one point it ran out of supplies and placed a notice in the window appealing for more. The *Millom News* of 4 February 1922 said:

All clothing for necessitous children has been distributed. Many of the Millom kiddies were disappointed as the consignments, generous as they were, did not suffice for the large number of applications. Money to feed and clothe the families of the unemployed in Millom came not from the government but from local resources supplied through the Bootle Board of Guardians.

In 1922 single unemployed men had to get by on 10 shillings (50p) a week if they were in lodgings or 7/6d (37p) if they lived with their parents. A *Millom News* report of 21 October 1922 quoted a board member saying: 'He knew of some men who were almost naked and who were quite unable to pay their way.' Many jobless men looked elsewhere for work and emigration to Canada, the United States, South Africa, South America and Australia was a popular choice – particularly for miners.

Stockings for the World

Millom was once a supplier of women's stockings and tights of national importance. One of the leading British manufacturers was Elbeo, which employed more than 400 people at Mainsgate Road. Perhaps the firm's biggest day in Millom came on Friday, 9 January 1970 when its new factory was officially opened. The story was reported in the Millom News:

Egremont Street, Millom, in the 1950s. Its unmade road would have been typical of most Millom streets in the Victorian building boom years.

Elbeo Manufacturing Ltd today celebrated the official opening of their new factory in Mainsgate Road, Millom. The opening was performed by Mr Thomas Urwin, MP, minister of state with special responsibility for Northern Region affairs.

Guest of honour at the opening was Mr Herman Bahner, the head of Elbeo International in Germany, who attended with several members of the Bahner family, descendants of the founders of the firm which first started manufacturing in Germany in 1748.

Also present were members of Elbeo management from both the Millom factory and the sales headquarters in Nottingham, and representative of local industrial, government and educational interests.

The factory was designed by Messrs Eberlin and Partners, architects, of Nottingham, in co-operation with GIA consulting engineers of Munich, and built by John Laing Construction Ltd, of Carlisle, and all three firms were represented among today's guests.

Also present at the opening were all the sales representatives and agents covering the British Isles, who have been taking part in Elbeo's half-yearly sales conference yesterday and today. The firm also exports to over 20 countries abroad, and several of Elbeo's overseas agents, who are responsible for the excellent and ever-increasing export figures, were also in attendance.

The opening of this new factory marks another milestone in the development of Elbeo, who began manufacturing in Millom in 1959, when their range of products consisted only of stockings – the famous Sup-hose support stockings and a separate line of conventional stockings.

Right: *A machine busy making stockings at the Millom Nylon Factory in Mainsgate Road.*

Below: *A worker at Millom Nylon Factory linking up the stockings.*

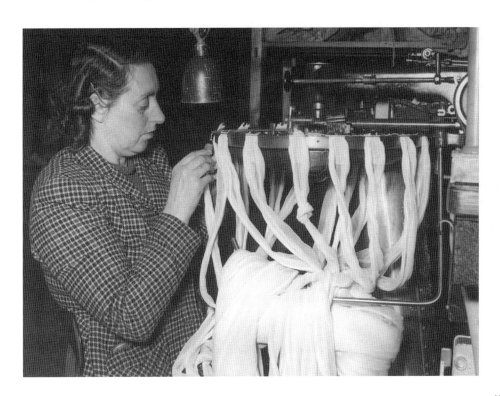

Above: *The Edwardian wool shop of H. White & Sons, Wellington Street, Millom. They were hosiers and woollen drapers.*

Opposite above: *The interior of Millom's first cycle repair shop, around 1910.*

Opposite below: *Shops in Millom Market Square in 1967 included Wadeson's newsagents, Blackburn's electrical store and Harris the chemist.*

The total number of employees at this time was 86, but this figure has now multiplied more than six times, with the current number of employees standing at 520, of whom 420 work at Millom, and the remaining 100 are either at the sales headquarters in Nottingham or spread about the country.

Co-operative Trading

One of the biggest commercial employers in Millom was the Co-operative Society. It was established in 1870 at Holborn Hill but by 1887 it had changed its name to Millom Co-operative Society to reflect the growth of Millom Newtown.

In 1888 the society built its new base at the top of Wellington Street for £5,253. It was a modern department store with an 800-seat public hall above. By 1894 the society had added branches at Albert Street and Main Street, Haverigg.

The Co-operative Directory for 1951 showed the wide range of activities undertaken at Millom for the society's 2,749 members. There were production departments for baking, confectionery, slaughtering, meat preparation, farming, shoe, boot and clog repairing and millinery.

The society acted as a distributor for grocery, bread, meat, greengrocery, fruit, milk, confectionery, drapery, millinery, jewellery, outfitting, shoes and boots, hardware, ironmongery, earthenware and crockery, furnishing and coal.

The Millom Co-operative Society collapsed in a blaze of national publicity in 1969 as a direct result of the closure of the town's biggest employer, Millom Ironworks. The shock news was reported in the North West Evening Mail *of 19 August 1969 under the headline 'End for Millom Co-op'. It said:*

Millom Co-operative Society, crippled by the closure of the town's ironworks last year, is to go into voluntary liquidation and an official guarantee that all investors will get their money back could not be given today.

In a bid to salvage enough funds to repay investors, some of whom put their life savings into the organisation, the society is putting its six branch shops and central three-storey block on a property market which has remained somewhat stagnant since the town's major industry shut down. The society has currently 2,750 shareholders, 15 per cent of whom hold 90 per cent of the investment capital.

Mr J. Myall, secretary of the society explained today that the closure of Millom Ironworks, leading to a flood of withdrawals from the investment capital had forced the society to ban further withdrawals and to start negotiating for a possible merger with the Barrow or Ulverston Co-operative societies as a survival policy.

Mr Myall said: 'Any question of amalgamation has been turned down flatly by the Barrow and Ulverston societies and the consequence is that we are now going into voluntary liquidation. As to the outcome for investors; this is where I hope we will be treated sympathetically. Nobody can possibly tell you what the final outcome will be. The assets are tied up in stock and it depends upon how much is realised for this as to how much can be paid out in the end. If we can realise anything like the value of the buildings the members could get a real bonus; these matters are imponderable.'

Mr Myall said that the society's biggest asset was property and already inquiries about one or two of the branch shops had been received. The biggest property, the central block in Wellington Street included the town's only cinema, rented from the society, was

Opposite: *Millom Co-operative Society's headquarters, public hall and department store on the corner of Wellington Street and Crown Street, c. 1940.*

Right: *Millom Co-operative Society's head office in Wellington Street, c. 1908.*

being priced down for the property market, said Mr Myall. He said, however: 'It should sell because of its site value. It is in the plumb-centre of the town.'

A meeting of shareholders on 23 September will formally pass a resolution to liquidate the society's assets and 40 employees of the society, comprising 18 men and 22 women and girls, will be given a month's notice.

Mr Myall said: 'In some cases people have put their life savings into the society. This is one of the tragedies of it, but we will definitely do our best in the interests of these people. The ironworks debacle put the finishing touches to this society. There was a flood of withdrawals and this absolutely put the cat among the pigeons.'

A few former Millom Ironworks' employees had invested their redundancy money in the society. Empty shops in Millom were evidence of the slow property market. A former drapers' shop stands empty near the Co-op central block in Wellington Street and there is an empty fruiterer's shop at a nearby corner.

Liquidation rumours have been circulating in the town for several weeks, so today's news did not come as a complete surprise to many people. The atmosphere in the town was one of waiting – and hoping.

'That's all we can do,' said 81-year-old Mr W.J. Rowe, of Grammerscroft. Mr Rowe, who has invested a little each week into the society, added: 'Perhaps they will manage to pay everyone out in full.'

A reassuring note was struck by Mr A. Davies, a member of the parish council, a rural district councillor and a member of the Co-op committee. He said: 'I can safely say this – I have no fear. I feel practically sure that the holdings of the shareholders will be respected and will be met in full. That is what I believe. I still want to look on the bright side of this.'

Millom Sparks National Crisis

Such was the impact of the collapse of Millom Co-operative Society that it had a near-disastrous ripple effect throughout the country as people in completely unrelated societies tried to cash in their investments. This effect was made much worse by a television programme which resulted in panic. The North West Evening Mail *of 4 November 1969 reported on the crisis. It said:*

A BBC programme about the closure of Millom Co-operative Society is causing Co-op members up and down the country to withdraw money from their local societies, alleged a Co-operative official in Manchester today. And Mr Jack Myall, secretary of the ill-fated Millom society, described the programme as vicious and irresponsible.

The Co-operative Wholesale Society in Manchester and Glasgow, together with the Co-operative Union, announced last night that they have sent a strong protest to the chairman and director general of the BBC about the Millom programme, which was shown last Thursday in the *Nationwide* show.

They have accused the BBC of deliberately creating false impressions about Co-operative societies. The programme, say the Co-op bosses, highlighted the misfortunes of the Millom Society in such a way as to cast reflections on the financial stability of Co-operative societies throughout the country.

The BBC has been asked to consider immediate action to mitigate the serious consequences of the presentation. A deputation of Co-op leaders is to meet Lord Hill tomorrow to discuss remedial action.

A statement issued by the Co-op said: 'The programme has quite unjustifiably aroused fears amongst Co-operative members as to the safety of their capital invested in societies. However, the good sense of Co-operative members in not being stampeded by the BBC is being confirmed by available evidence that they generally refuse to believe that their own co-operatives are in the same unfortunate position as the Millom Co-op

'This (Millom) is a unique situation, not true of the country as a whole, and it is therefore grossly unfair that the BBC should have gone out of its way to deliberately create false impressions about Co-operative societies generally.

'The Co-operative Union's regional plan is specifically designed to avoid these casualties by encouraging small Co-ops to merge with powerful neighbouring societies. This plan is moving quickly, and its progress will be the best safeguard against a recurrence of the Millom experience.'

The programme, introduced by Mr Michael Barrett, included interviews with members who faced the loss of part of their savings. Mr R. Southern, general secretary of the Co-operative Union, said at his Manchester office today: 'Somebody is in for the chopper at the BBC.'

Buffing leather with the help of emery paper at the Millom Tannery.

Millom's New Tannery

One of the new industries to West Cumberland hit badly by industrial recession was a leather tannery. It was built on land next to the River Lazy, close to Haverigg. The Millom News *of 30 April 1938, described the start to building work on the new project. It said:*

The foundation stone of the new Millom Tannery, which is being erected by the West Cumberland Industrial Development Company Ltd, was laid on Thursday afternoon by Mr Frank Anderson, MP for the Whitehaven Division. A large crowd gathered at the site, near Haverigg, and the laying of the stone was greeted by great cheers.

Mr R. Crichton, chairman of the company, said the stone-laying ended the very long and difficult negotiations necessary before the scheme could materialise, and the end of efforts by a great many people privately and publicly, the Special Areas Reconstruction Association, the Nuffield Trust, the Cumberland Development Council and the West Cumberland Industrial Development Company.

Mr Anderson had been very active all the time to secure the new tannery. Mr Anderson, who was presented with a trowel made by the Goldsmiths and Silversmiths Company, London, said the tannery would not be a small place. Perhaps in the near future other industries would follow.

He could assure the people of Millom and Haverigg, who had had such a bitter time in the past five years, that the tannery was the forerunner of other new industries.

The new tannery is to be operated by the West Coast Chrome Tannery Co. Ltd, for the manufacture of smooth chrome leather. It will be a single storey, steel framed brick building covering 51,400sq.ft; 460ft long and 110ft broad. The erection is to be completed in six months and will employ 200 men and youths.

Left: *Workers at Millom Tannery ironing or electrifying sheepskins as part of the process to convert the wool into fur.*

Opposite: *Millom stationmaster Frank Cope, pictured in the 1950s.*

Speeches at the luncheon which followed at the West County Hotel, Millom, were made by Mr Crichton, Mr Anderson, Major A. Hibbert, chairman of the Cumberland Development Council and Mr Morris S. Gibbs CBE, managing director of the Special Areas Reconstruction Association.

Independent Gas Supplier

Millom no longer has a gasworks and receives its supplies direct by pipe rather than through the traditional giant gas holders facing down Queen Street. This is how the North Western Daily Mail *of Wednesday, 31 March, 1954, reported the last day of work at the furnaces which made Millom's gas long before natural gas was taken from Morecambe Bay.*

At 4.30 p.m. yesterday afternoon, watched by Mr P.R. Dawson, district manager, Mr F.C. Buckley, group production engineer, and a number of workmates, Mr James Woodburn drew the last charge at Millom Gasworks prior to their closure.

Mr Woodburn actually retired last year after 39 years' service at the gasworks, but he came along yesterday afternoon to perform the ceremony he had carried out so often, only this time with a feeling of nostalgia.

From now on Millom will be supplied with its gas by pipeline from Barrow, where, last week, Mr D.P. Welman, chairman of the North Western Gas Board, instituted the service. Workmates stood by yesterday as Mr Woodburn, who began his career at the gasworks in 1914, drew the final charge from the furnace.

After the charge had been drawn, Mr John Young, who has upwards of 30 years' service at the gasworks, turned off the exhauster which pumps the gas into the holders and Millom began to draw its gas from Barrow under the scheme which has cost the North Western Gas Board £73,000.

To complete the Millom scheme, 10 miles of eight inch diameter main were laid alongside the railway line to connect up with the existing main at Askam.

The railway played a major role in the development of Millom and until the 1960s the area was criss-crossed with industrial rail tracks taking iron ore and pig iron to Millom pier for shipment or to Millom railway station sidings.

Passenger and goods transport also relied heavily on the speed and reliability of the railways. For many hundreds of workers arriving to make a new life in Millom the railway station must have been their first view of a rapidly-expanding town.

The station had its own goods yard and warehouse, now the Safeway supermarket and car park, its own ticket office, waiting rooms and uniformed stationmaster.

On 1 November 1975, a special ceremony was held at Millom railway station to mark the 125th anniversary of the rail link being established between Whitehaven and Barrow.

The grand opening of the Whitehaven and Furness Junction Railway took place on 1 November 1850, when two special trains from Whitehaven and Barrow met at Broughton. Directors and their guests celebrated the occasion in the Old King's Head.

It took another seven years to complete the coastal railway link from Barrow to Lancaster. In 1850 the station at Millom was called Holborn Hill.

The station has seen its share of excitement over the years. In 1904 a large crowd of spectators came to see damage caused to the passenger footbridge by a goods train carrying two huge boilers from the Lonsdale Ironworks at Whitehaven. The steam valve on one of the boilers caught the decking of the bridge and almost pulled it over.

On 20 February 1913 a passenger train from Barrow was being shunted into sidings when a goods train from Whitehaven crashed into the back of it. The back coach toppled over into the Millom signal box. One of the Furness railway locomotives was derailed and fell on its side next to the track. The signal box was badly damaged and a signalman called Mr Holmes was injured.

Above: *Inside the former Millom Crown post office at Lapstone Road, Millom, in 1969.*

Left: *A Cumberland Motors bus crew with their double-decker outside the old depot on the corner of Market Street and Lonsdale Road around 1953. The depot is now a car showroom for W. Milligan & Sons. On the left is a coal wagon in the former Millom station yard, now a sports hall.*

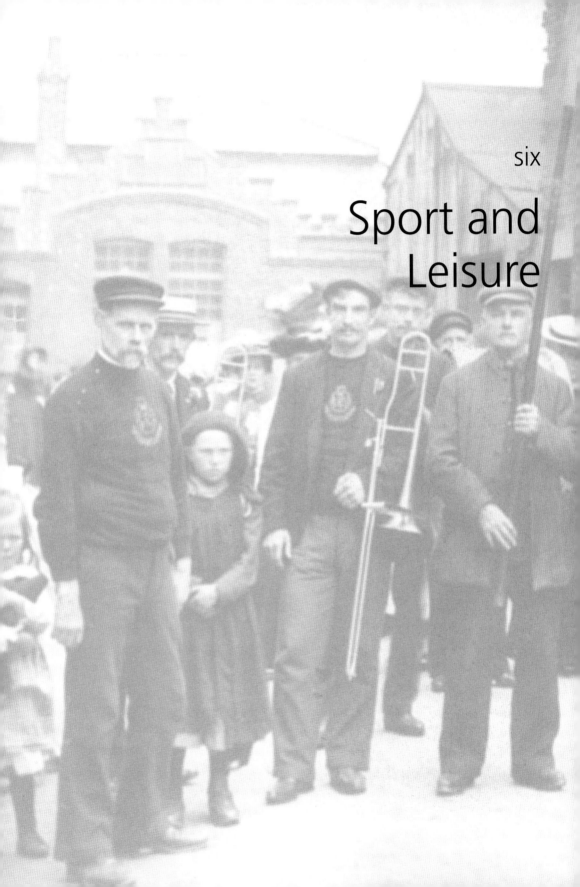

six

Sport and Leisure

No sport can match rugby in Millom for length of tradition and level of success. Millom Rugby League Club was founded in 1873 and is recognised as the oldest amateur rugby club in the world.

The club was formed to play rugby union and did so with great success. In 1885 Millom had a team in the Cumberland County Union and played in the County Challenge Cup competition. By 1887 Millom was starting to be a force to be reckoned with – winning the County Challenge Cup and keeping it for the following two years. Between 1887 and 1895 the Millom club won seven trophies.

A total of twenty-two northern clubs broke away from the English Rugby Union on 29 August 1895, over the issue of 'broken time' payments made to men who had lost earnings in order to play. They formed the Northern Union which became Rugby League in 1922.

By 1897 Millom had joined Barrow, Ulverston and Lancaster in the Northern Union. The town continued its production line of great players, many finding fame with the big clubs of Yorkshire and Lancashire.

Sammy Northmore started with Millom when it was still a rugby union club. As a union player he won a cap for England in 1897 against Ireland in Dublin and was in the Cumberland side which lost the County Championship final to Kent the same year.

As a league player, he was captain of the first Cumberland Northern Union team, which lost to Yorkshire at Hunslet in 1898. It was then a 15-a-side game and Millom provided twelve members of the county side. The same year he captained Millom to the Lancashire Second Competition Championship.

Millom-born full-back and centre Bill Eagers played for Millom and Haverigg in the 1890s but found fame with Bradford and Hunslet. He won twenty caps with Cumberland and made a single appearance for England in 1906. Bill played in the Challenge Cup, Yorkshire Cup and Championship winning Hunslet team of 1907/08. He was badly wounded in German East Africa during the First World War.

The Millom brothers Jim and Dick Clampitt both made their mark as forwards for Cumberland. Jim made his Millom debut against South Shields in 1903 and played the first of twenty-three games as a forward for Cumberland against Lancashire at Wigan in 1905. In those days Millom played in the second division of the Northern League. He was in the winning county teams against both the New Zealand and Australian tourists and by 1909 made his winning England debut against Wales.

His brother Dick started his playing career with Millom in 1904 before trying soccer at Barrow and rugby league with Broughton Rangers and Cumberland. He was a Challenge Cup winner in 1911 as a forward for Broughton against Wigan and won nine county caps.

John Coulson of Lonsdale Road, Millom, signed for Hunslet in 1924 and won eighteen caps for Cumberland, starting in 1925. His record still stands of four tries in a match for Cumberland against Yorkshire to win his second County Championship medal in 1932. He played a total of 273 games for Hunslet, up to September 1932, and six games for Halifax. In later years as a policeman at Leeds he often patrolled the touchline for matches at Headingley.

Syd Walmsley was lucky to ever pull on a Millom rugby shirt. He was wounded in both legs serving with the Coldstream Guards during the First World War. Syd joined Millom in 1920 and played wing, centre or full-back. His impact in Millom's losing Challenge Cup first round tie at Leeds that year was such that the big Yorkshire club snapped him up.

Millom rugby league player Syd Walmsley.

He earned Yorkshire Cup and Challenge Cup winner's medals. After 188 games he left for Huddersfield in 1925. He played for England twice in 1924 and won twelve Cumberland caps.

Millom amateur at both league and union, Les Bettinson, was persuaded to sign as a professional for Salford manager Gus Risman in 1957. The back played twelve years for Salford in 317 full appearances. He was top try scorer with eleven in 1966/67. He won seven caps for Cumberland and was a county champion in 1965/66 and 1966/67. He retired as a player in 1969 and as Salford coach he took the club to victory in the 1974/75 BBC2 Floodlit Trophy over Warrington.

In more recent years a crowd of 4,000 came to the Millom club's Devonshire Road ground to see the home team lose in a great struggle against professionals Hunslet in the first round of the Rugby League Challenge Cup in 1973. In 1986 Millom reached the final of the BARLA Whitbread Trophy at Headingley, Leeds, losing to Myson, of Hull.

Rugby or Emigration

One of Millom's finest rugby players was almost lost to the game. Bill Eagers was packed and ready to emigrate to South Africa but the outbreak of what became known as the Boer War gave him second thoughts. The decision to stay in England was made easier by a lucrative offer to play for leading Northern Union club Bradford. The Millom Gazette of 27 July 1900 told the story under the headline 'Millom Footballer for Bradford':

The clever full-back of the Millom Football Club, William Eagers, has been secured by the Bradford Football Club for the coming season. Eagers had made arrangements to emigrate to South Africa and had everything prepared to leave England in the course of a fortnight.

The West Coast Tannery Vigodney Cup winners at cricket in 1949. From left to right, back row: J. Boundy, T. Shoyelton, J. Procter, S. Warren, C. Evans (scorer), R. Myers, J. Scott, D. Rowe, E. Burrows. Front row: I. Evans, J. Heap (professional), A. Vicodny, G. Wilson (captain), A. Harris, E. Fallows, B. Taylor.

The continued unsatisfactory state of affairs in that country, however, caused him to postpone his journey.

In the meantime, some Bradfordians paid a visit to Millom, and the inducements held out to secure the services of such a clever exponent of football are said to have been quite as tempting as any prospective position or pecuniary advantage in South Africa.

Of course, before Eagers is allowed to don the Bradford jersey, a pecuniary consideration will have to be made to the Millom club.

Batting For Records

Millom Cricket Club has had great success in recent years, including a memorable run as Division 1 champions of the North Lancashire & District Cricket League from 1989 to 1993, but perhaps the club's finest single performance came in June 1923 when an amazing 414 runs were scored against Furness team Vickerstown in a frantic four-and-a-quarter hours.

The mighty score came in the second round of the Higson Cup played at Vickerstown. The demoralised home team were bowled out for just 59 the following night. The two Doidges opened for Millom, scoring 74 and 43. After them came Maurice Gill, the club professional, who helped himself to 77 runs. Next up was club captain Alec Rigg who hit 119 not out.

Herbert Thomas and J. Ralph were both bowled by Youren for a duck. The next highest score came from the extras – no fewer than 55. At that time Vickerstown were captained by George Mudge whose cousin Syd was playing for Millom.

An undated picture of Millom Cricket Club players. From left to right, back row: Harold Peter, Tom Whithicombe, Herbert Thomas, Charles Peter, Tom Fawcett, Eric Davis. Front row: Alf Doidge, Will Allen, Alec Rigg, Sid Mudge, Maurice Gill, Will Ormandy.

This shows the Mackereths Cricket Club, winners of the Millom Knockout Competition in 1947. From left to right, back row: A. Mackereth, S. Fallows, W. Magee, T. Edmondson, J. Waugh, J. Taylor, G. Grimshaw. Front row: W. Hortop, I. Evans, W. H. Dawson (captain) L. Todd, W.R. Wall.

The Holborn Hill Royal Brass Band in concert.

Brass Band Contest

Brass bands were a traditional part of life in industrial northern towns. Millom and Haverigg has produced several bands over the years with Hoborn Hill Royal Brass Band being the oldest and best known. Bands frequently travelled to neighbouring towns for concerts or to take part in contests. The Millom Gazette of 23 July 1892 reported on a contest held in the town. It said:

We regret that we cannot report an unqualified success for the brass band contest at Millom on Saturday last. The bill of fare was not very attractive, the price (one shilling) was somewhat prohibitive, and the weather was not in accordance with the best traditions of the month of July.

With these three adverse circumstances perhaps it was only natural there should have been something resembling failure, and when we state that the takings at the gate amounted to but £25 whilst more than that was given in prizes, it will be seen that the promoters must necessarily have found themselves considerably out of pocket by the venture.

The contest was held in the Millom football field and the bands entering were Barrow Steelworks, Millom Wesleyans, Derwent Iron and Steelworks, Workington, Haverigg Band, Roose Band and Barrow Borough Band.

There were four prizes offered for the selection contest and two for the quick step. The latter was decided first, all the bands entering for it.

Each band had to march from the top of the railway bridge to the Station Hotel. The first prize was won by the Haverigg Band and the second by the Barrow Steelworks.

The prizes in the selection contest were won as follows: First prize, Barrow Steelworks, conductor Mr Wood – test piece, selection from Mozart; second prize,

The Millom Salvation Army band in Nelson Street, during the Edwardian era.

Millom Wesleyan, conductor Mr E.F. Birkenshaw – test piece, selection from Weber; third prize, Derwent Iron and Steelworks Band (Workington), conductor Mr Rimmer – test piece, selection from Mozart; fourth prize Haverigg Band, conductor Mr Heap – test piece, selection from Mozart. The judge was Mr J. Ainsworth, professor of music, Chorley.

Previous to the selection contest, Mr W.G. Hurst, the well-known bicycle-trick rider, gave some exceedingly interesting exhibitions of his skill, his feats including a descent of some steps on a single bicycle wheel and riding upon a cart wheel.

A special train was run from Ulverston, calling at intermediate stations, which brought a large number of people into the town. After the judge's declaration, dancing was indulged on the field, music being provided by the Holborn Hill Royal Brass Band, which was debarred from taking part in the contest.

Junior Football Winners

The North West Evening Mail *of Thursday 9 May 1929 reported on the junior football success of the Lapstone Road Scholars.*
A 60 guineas championship cup was presented to the Millom Lapstone Road schoolboys' team, winners of the Millom Association Football League, on Wednesday. Mr J. Sharpe, principal of the Millom Secondary School, complimented the new champions (the secondary school had won the championship last year).

It was rather unique, he said, for Mr Morton, the Lapstone Road headmaster, to receive an Association Football cup, because he (Mr Morton) was usually on the winning side in rugby football competitions.

A Millom Celtic soccer player,
c. 1910.

Alderman J. Flynn JP CC, was pleased to be present to hand the cup to the champions, for he had won his first football prize on that field. He had a great admiration for rugby football, because Millom had so many times reached the top at that code, and he was of the opinion that the Millom club, if it had stuck to rugby, would still be one of the best teams in the North of England.

He was very glad that Lapstone Road (elementary school team) had recently defeated the secondary school. It showed that there was some grit down at the bottom as well as in 'their fancy schools.'

Mr Morton, in receiving the cup for Lapstone Road, also expressed his preference for rugby football, although he was proud to receive that cup.

The presentation took place after a Champions v Rest of League match, in which the champions were beaten by three goals to two. Fallows scored two goals and Sheldon one for the Rest of League team: the Lapstone Road scorers being Williamson and Edmondson.

Swimming Pool for Haverigg

The 1930s were a time of uncertain employment and Millom council was among many looking for schemes funded with public money to generate employment. One suggestion was a swimming pool for Haverigg and the prospects were reported in the Millom News *on Saturday, 1 February 1936.*

By an overwhelming vote of 253 against 17, the ratepayers of Millom consented to the parish council levying a penny rate to cover the engineer's fees for the proposed Haverigg swimming pool.

Approximately 300 people were present at the Market Hall on Monday evening, when the chair was taken by the chairman of the council Mr S. Park. Before the commencement of the business a silence in respect of the late King George was observed.

The chairman said that the rate was needed to pay for the engineer's fees, so that details of the proposed scheme could be sent to the Ministry of Health for their consideration.

A generous grant had been promised by the commissioner for the Special Area of West Cumberland, Mr St Clare Grondona. The scheme had been on the go for some time and was, at a recent meeting, withdrawn on the grounds that the council were unable, in the event of the commissioner not giving a grant, to bear the cost of the fees. At a resultant meeting with the commissioner's secretary, it was stated that a grant would be made.

The grant of a sum of money to cover the whole of the cost of the non-revenue making part of the scheme would be made, while a grant to cover a certain amount less a sum of equivalent to less than a penny rate would be made. He would propose the resolution.

In seconding, Councillor Martindale said that it was necessary that something should be done for Haverigg. A voice asked: 'How much will the upkeep be?' The chairman: '"Nothing. We are going to make it a paying proposition." (Laughter and applause).

The clerk, Mr W.N. Kitchin, said the total approximate yearly expenditure would be £124. The total cost would be somewhere in the neighbourhood of £5,000, and the commissioner was going to make a grant for nearly that figure. The engineer's fees were returnable in the grant.

Cries of 'sit down' and 'shut up' greeted a voice who said that he did not want a swimming pool. The chairman said that if they did not do something for Haverigg, the village would become a white elephant. They had a public park, and before they laid out the bowling green, that was a white elephant.

Councillor Floyd said that the grant was one of the best they had ever had, and it would be for the benefit of the whole district. Unless they secured a penny rate, the council could not do anything. 'It's a penny in the slot,' said Mr Floyd, 'and I hope that the meter will work right.'

A show of hands was then made and on a count it was found that 253 people were in favour of the council levying a penny rate, while 17 voted against the proposition. The tellers were Messrs M. Kirkby, W.N. Kitchin, L. Williams, J.F. Irwin, and others. The result was greeted by a storm of cheering and applause.

A Fool and His Money

Today electric gaming machines for fun or for cash prizes are a standard fixture in almost all public houses. Back in 1966 Millom's councillors were holding out against this new form of small-scale gambling. The latest battle by Millom Rural District Council was reported in the Evening Mail *on Tuesday, 18 January in 1966 under the headline 'Ban on 'not Bandit' machines'.*

Pleas for amusement machines to be allowed in two Millom public houses were rejected yesterday by Millom RDC's finance and general purposes committee.

A representative of Thompson's Brewery made the application for the Plough Inn, Holborn Hill and the Devonshire Hotel. He said the machines should not be referred to as 'one-armed bandits' as they gave the operator an 80 per cent chance of having his coin returned.

They would be installed on a licence basis under the name of the licensee. Through a new Gambling Act, they could not return more than one shilling (5p) cash or five shillings-worth (25p) of tokens. This takes out the gambling element because the winnings are limited. The machines should be regarded as amusement, for there is no danger of corruption.

Replying to a question from the committee chairman Councillor F.G. Wilson, the representative said the machines could not be tampered with and were serviced regularly.

Demanding that both applications should be turned down, Councillor L.J. Sawrey said: 'This is our opportunity to discourage gambling in a form which often goes to great extremes.'

Said Councillor Peter Cross: 'This is a totally different case from others we have dealt with. It is no different to someone selling a raffle ticket, and to debar the machines on the grounds that they corrupt teenagers would be totally unfair.'

Councillor W.M. Brayton's view was: 'Although I am against gambling, this is not the worst type of gambling device.'

Councillor E. McDonnell said the machines were identical with others refused by the committee.

New Club for Boys

A new social club was opened for Millom boys in former stables at Nelson Street in 1936. The opening ceremony was reported in the Millom News *on 19 December. It said:*

Mr W.F. Sadler, CC, chairman of the Cumberland Development Council, officially opened a new boys club in connection with St James' (RC) church and Institute on Wednesday evening. There was a large attendance. The club has been converted from old stables and is situated in Nelson Street.

The club was sponsored by the Revd Father Hayward, the popular priest at St James', and is for the benefit of all boys. Father Hayward was the chairman, and others on the platform were Mr Sadler, Mr J. Sharpe and Commander M. Murray (of the Cumberland and Westmorland Association of Boys Clubs).

Commander Murray spoke on the value of boys clubs and hoped that Millom would set an example that other districts would follow. Father Hayward had worked very hard for the new club, and he hoped it would be a success.

'If you want to have a good soul you must have a good body,' said Father Hayward.

It was somewhere where the boys could go and enjoy themselves and do something different. There would be physical training, etc., and they would be taught how to take care of themselves.

Preparations to be a good citizen was the aim of the club, and to have a good healthy body and a good soul was the way to attaining the aim. He hoped it would be a success, but if it was not he had another arrow for his bow.

Many a woman would be wondering if there was something for the girls, and he could assure them that he had a scheme for the girls. That would come later.

They had made a start on the boys club. The furnishing, etc, was to come later, and he hoped the public would support the venture financially.

Mr Sadler, opening the club, said he was honoured to do so. He and the late Father Kelly were very intimate friends, and his death had been a very great blow to him. He could say that the St James' parishioners were very fortunate in getting such an excellent successor as Father Hayward, whom he wished every success.

Mr Sadler said he never thought such a splendid club could have been made out of the old stables, and it was up to everyone, now that the club had been started, to back Father Hayward in all that had been done.

It could only lead to the good of the boys, and was practically the first in the county.

Fame on the Radio

A Millom opera singer made headlines in the Millom News *on 3 December 1938, when the opportunity arose to make a BBC radio broadcast. It said:*

'Queen Elizabeth' from the Millom Amateur Operatic Society's production of Merrie England in November 1912.

Mr J. Woodruff, of Devonshire Road, Millom, is to broadcast from the Manchester Studio of the BBC on Friday 3 June, when a special operatic programme will be relayed.

Mr Woodruff is a baritone singer of outstanding quality, and has delighted South Cumbrians during the many years he has been behind the footlights. He has been a member of the Millom Amateur Operatic Society since its inception in 1910 and has taken the male lead in each production ever since.

Mr Woodruff will sing the 'Fisherman's Song' from the *Rebel King*, one of the productions of the Millom society in which he took part – and will sing other songs new to him.

It is a great honour for Mr Woodruff, not merely from the broadcasting point of view but because he has been selected from such a wide area. At the audition some weeks ago, those who were tested by BBC musical experts came from places as far apart as Chester and Carlisle.

Mr Tommy Burns, another member of the Millom society, recently had the honour of singing on the air. He took part in a special Cumbrian programme, Hark Forrard, which was relayed from the Newcastle studio.

Best in Britain

Many events were held in 1951 to make the Festival of Britain. It was supposed to mark the end of years of hardship and shortage following the Second World War. A whole series of celebrations were held in Millom but one local musician went to London to make his mark. The Barrow News *of Saturday, 23 June described the success of Robert Latimer under the headline 'Won brass title in London':*

Mr Robert Latimer, a café proprietor of 102 Market Street, Millom, won the Festival of Britain Class for Brass Instruments in the contest which took place at the Wigmore Hall, London, on Tuesday. He gained 90 marks out of a possible 100 and was three marks ahead of the runners-up.

Mr Latimer qualified for the national final by winning the area championships for brass instruments at Whitehaven Musical Festival in February.

He is a former member of Barrow Shipyard Band and of Barrow Salvation Army Band.

Of Mr Latimer's performance, Mr Harry Mortimer and Dr F. Staton commented on his beautiful tone and style and said that although he was not entirely without fault, they were very impressed by some brilliant playing.

Mr Latimer, who plays the euphonium, started playing at the age of 13.

No Play on Sundays

Nothing much happened on Sundays in Millom and Haverigg during the 1950s beyond going to church. Councillors were keen to keep it that way when a bid was made to let children play in the pleasure grounds at Haverigg. The North Western Evening Mail *of Wednesday, 2 June 1954, told the story under the headline 'Children should be taught to observe Sunday':*

Millom Parish Council last night threw out a proposal to open the children's section of the pleasure ground at Haverigg on Sundays. Opening the discussion, Councillor T. Wilson said he had been approached by numerous people for the pleasure ground to be

A St George's parish church billiards team from the 1950s. On the back row is Alf Mackereth (left), a well-known Millom sweet shop owner.

open. He pointed out that many people visited the village during the summer and there was nothing for the children to do. He could see no harm in it.

Support came from Councillor W. Bickerstaffe, who said Haverigg was purely and simply a seaside resort. An attendant was there at present to look after things. It could be argued that if Haverigg were opened, Millom would have to follow, but that did not apply.

Opposing, Councillor Mrs M.A. Knox urged the council not to be like a lot of puppets and dance to the whim of a few people in Haverigg. She was one who liked to observe Sundays and children should be taught to do the same. There were plenty of other places to play.

If they were to be an example, could they lead the children into not observing Sundays? Haverigg, she contended, would be a lever for the opening of the pleasure ground at Millom. She told councillors that if the proposal were approved it would be a false step.

Councillor A.E. Elwood also opposed the suggestion. Councillor H.O. Bannen felt 'it is wrong.'

Councillor L. Wilson, in favour, said it had never been opened because of antiquated ideas and Councillor S. Park thought if the playground was opened the parents would suffer through having to buy more clothes.

Summing up, Councillor T. Wilson said he had brought forward the proposal at the request of the people of Haverigg.

The proposal was defeated by seven votes to five, three members abstaining.

Above: *The Haverigg Unemployed Male Voice choir in the 1930s. Many social groups were started during the depression years to provide an interest for men who had known nothing but regular employment.*

Opposite above: *St James' Catholic Institute billiard team with its championship trophy, c. 1910. The players include C. Coulter, Peter O'Hare, Jimmy Burns, James Wilkinson, John Rogan and A. Bickerdike.*

Opposite below: *Millom Mixed Voice Choir, who were shield winners in around 1923.*

Other local titles published by Tempus

Barrow-in-Furness Remembered
BILL MYERS

Barrow-in-Furness has experienced an astonishing transformation from a village to a major industrial town over the past 150 years. This book reveals the stories behind this growth through contemporary newspaper headlines and reports. Digging for iron, steelmaking, shipbuilding, the growth of the railways and the laying of tram lines are described in articles and historical notes drawn from a number of newspapers once published in the town.
0 7524 2083 6

Barrow Raiders Rugby League Club
KEITH NUTTER

Spanning the decades, this book recounts the story of Barrow Raiders Rugby League Club from its formation in 1875 through to the present day. Illustrated with over 200 photographs this volume includes details about many of the memorable matches in which Barrow has featured as well as the players to have worn the Barrow colours down the years.
0 7524 2702 4

Workington
RICHARD L.M. BYERS

This volume traces some of the developments that have occurred in the West Cumbrian town of Workington during the last century. Over 170 archive images highlight the importance of local industry in the town, including coal mining and the shipbuilding, which employed several generations of townspeople. Later, the town became a major centre for the production of iron and steel, and as a result Victorian Workington grew dramatically.
0 7524 3295 8

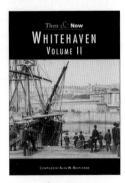

Whitehaven Then & Now Volume II
ALAN ROUTLEDGE

This collection of over 85 pairs of images reveals some of the changes that have taken place in Whitehaven during the last century. Streets and buildings, organisations, shops and churches are shown as they used to be. Each pair is accompanied by informative text containing historical detail and local information sure to appeal to both the long-established resident and the interested visitor.
0 7524 3094 7

If you are interested in purchasing other books published by Tempus, or in case you have difficulty finding any Tempus books in your local bookshop, you can also place orders directly through our website
www.tempus-publishing.com